Making MINNESOTA TERRITORY
1849–1858

ANNE R. KAPLAN *and* MARILYN ZIEBARTH, *editors*

SPECIAL ISSUE OF
MINNESOTA HISTORY

MINNESOTA HISTORICAL SOCIETY PRESS • ST. PAUL

MINNESOTA HISTORICAL SOCIETY PRESS
ST. PAUL 55102

∞ The paper used in this publication meets the minimum requirements of the
American National Standard for Information Sciences—Permanence for Printed
Library Materials, ANSI Z39.48-1984.

Manufactured in the United States of America
9 8 7 6 5 4 3 2

ISBN 0-87351-373-8 (paper)

Library of Congress Cataloging-in-Publication Data
Making Minnesota Territory, 1849-1858 / Anne R. Kaplan and Marilyn Ziebarth,
    editors.
        p. cm.
        Includes bibliographical references.
        ISBN 0-87351-373-8 (pbk. : alk. paper)
        1. Minnesota—History—To 1858. I. Kaplan, Anne R.
    II. Ziebarth, Marilyn.
    F606.M34 1999
    977.6'04—dc21   98-51071
                                                         CIP

FRONT COVER: Detail from Francis D. Millet's 6 x 10-foot oil painting, *The Treaty
of Traverse des Sioux,* depicting how the U.S. obtained much of southern Minnesota
from the Sisseton and Wahpeton Dakota. Millet's 1905 canvas, made from the
sketches of Frank B. Mayer, who had attended the 1851 treaty signing, hangs over
the fireplace in the Governor's Reception Room in the Minnesota State Capitol.
For the full painting, see "Territorial Imperative: How Minnesota Became the
32nd State." *Photograph by Jerry Mathiason.*

BACK COVER: *Fort Snelling* by Sgt. Edward K. Thomas, about 1850

INSIDE COVERS: *Winnebago Wigwams* by Seth Eastman, reproduced in Henry R.
Schoolcraft's *Indian Tribes of the United States* (1852), and the Snyder and
McFarlane land office, Minneapolis, 1856.

Contents

Mendota, about 1845

Preface

1999. 1849. One hundred and fifty years ago, in March 1849, Minnesota Territory was established by an act of Congress. Lines were drawn on a map enclosing lakes and rivers, prairie and woods, hills and valleys. Officials were appointed, local men grappled for power, and a European-American grid of law was officially imposed on the new entity. For some of Minnesota's residents, it was a time of great hope and wide-open opportunity. For the territory's native peoples—Ojibwe, Dakota, Ho-Chunk (Winnebago), Mandan, Hidatsa, and Arikara—and the métis, or European-Indian people of the fur trade, the outlook was far different. Their ways of life and livelihoods would change forever.

Anniversaries provide a time to rethink as well as to remember, and so the editors of *Minnesota History* invited an assortment of thoughtful writers to look back and reassess, from the edge of the new millennium, the meaning of the territory. How did its creation fit into the larger national picture at midcentury, especially the growing controversy over slavery? What did the political acts of boundary drawing and nation building mean for people's lives? Who lived in Minnesota before the territory was created, and what kinds of people moved to the region during the nine years before statehood in 1858? What induced newcomers to travel beyond the farthest rail connections to take up a new life in a new place? And what did this mean to the Indian and mixed-blood people who had lived in the region for centuries?

This collection of essays, issued simultaneously as a special edition of *Minnesota History* and as a book, is an attempt to answer to those questions—and more. Articles by Rhoda R. Gilman, Bruce M. White, William E. Lass, and Jane Lamm Carroll detail the varied people, the web of politics, the sometimes outrageous boosterism, and the always opinionated newspapers of Minnesota Territory. In "Every Object Tells a Story," Marcia Anderson, Patty Dean, Charles Diesen, Kendra Dillard, Lisa Krahn, Linda McShannock, Stephen Osman, and Adam Scher show that the variety of objects preserved in the collections of the Minnesota Historical Society—itself created with the territory in 1849—speak volumes about their owners and their era. Similarly, Scott Anfinson's "Territorial Views" unlocks the silent stories of some still-standing remnants of the territory's built environment. John Crippen and Katherine Piva detail MHS historic sites associated with the long-ago territorial years.

Finally, eight "Day in the Life" features scattered throughout this collection capture the vivid everyday sights, smells, sounds, and events familiar to some of Minnesota's early residents but largely lost to us now. The people and occurrences depicted are real, although the authors were granted some creative latitude in piecing together their stories. Here are found the voices of everyday citizens from many walks of life, suggesting the diversity of the territory.

Along with the authors, many people contributed greatly to this volume. For invaluable advice on both the big picture and the small details, thanks are due to Brian Horrigan, William E. Lass, and Alan Woolworth; for tireless and inspired illustration sleuthing, Deborah Swanson; for help selecting from the riches of the Minnesota Historical Society's unique images collection, Bonnie G. Wilson, and from its art collection, Thomas O'Sullivan; for facilitating "Every Object Tells a Story," including artifact selection, Sherri Gebert-Fuller and Kendra Dillard; for their artful work evident in these pages, photographers Peter Latner, Eric Mortenson, and Jerry Mathiason; for the maps, Alan Ominsky; for making a beautiful whole from the parts, designer Lois Stanfield; for careful and patient keying of corrections, Chris Banks; and for reading portions of this collection, the Minnesota Historical Society's Indian Advisory Committee members David Aubid, Jody Beaulieu, and Jeff Savage. The essays were funded, in part, by a grant from the research department of the Minnesota Historical Society with funds provided by the State of Minnesota.

—*Anne R. Kaplan & Marilyn Ziebarth*

TERRITORIAL IMPERATIVE

How Minnesota Became the 32nd S

RHODA R. GILMAN

tate

T he prairies and forests, the lakes and watersheds that surround the upper reaches of the Mississippi and Red Rivers, and the head of Lake Superior have been known and occupied by men and women for more than 10,000 years. During that span, the human and natural landscapes have been reworked several times by waves of climatic and cultural change. But none was swifter than the change that went into high gear as boundaries were drawn on a map and the region was named "Minnesota." That event occurred in March 1849, when a bill

Indian people at Mendota and soldiers across the Minnesota River at the dawn of the territorial era, portrayed in Henry Lewis's *Fort Snelling*, oil on canvas, about 1850

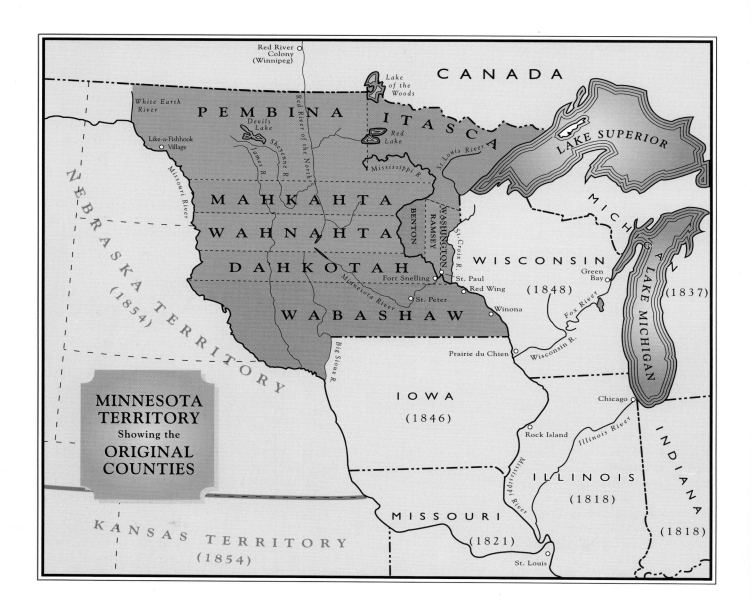

MINNESOTA
TERRITORY
Showing the
ORIGINAL
COUNTIES

creating the new territory was passed by the U.S. Senate and signed by President James K. Polk.[1]

For most Americans, whether their sense of history stems from the classroom or from Disneyland, 1849 is associated with the California gold rush. The fact that Minnesota came into being at the same time is not entirely unconnected. Both events were expressions of the burst of expansion that transformed the United States in the 1840s. As late as 1842, the Senate had seriously considered but ultimately rejected a treaty with the Dakota nation that would have created a permanent island of Indian residence and government in the region that was later to become southern Minnesota. The treaty promised the Dakota and other northern tribes that white immigrants would be excluded from the territory and that, after a short period of settled living, Indian people there would be granted United States citizenship along with their own territorial and,

ultimately, state government. The measure was urged by the war department, recommended by the president, and vigorously supported by Henry H. Sibley, the local representative of the American Fur Company.[2] Yet less than a decade later, Sibley was lobbying just as hard to organize the same region as a territory for European-American settlers instead. What had happened?

The seven years between 1842 and 1849 saw the United States assume continent-wide dominance as its "manifest destiny." A war upon Mexico was concluded in February 1848 with the taking of that country's northern frontier from Texas to California. Later in the same year, Oregon Territory was formed from a region that until 1844 had been jointly occupied with Britain. Thus, the entire configuration of the nation had changed, both on maps and in the minds of its citizens. No longer was the Mississippi River some sort of ultimate boundary. Linking the East Coast to the Far West had become a national priority, and the idea of placing between them a state that might differ in race and culture from others in the American republic—an idea never accepted by Congress— became unthinkable.

The 1840s had also seen the creation of two new states bordering the upper Mississippi region— Iowa in 1846 and Wisconsin in 1848. What was left of the two territories from which they had been carved straddled the headwaters of the great river and reached west to the Missouri River and north to the British possessions. Most of the land still belonged to the Dakota and Ojibwe tribes, and the scattered white population of traders, missionaries, government agents, and a few lumberjacks was far from the minimum of 5,000 required for territorial status—but the logic of national expansion called for the area to be organized immediately.

No one understood that fact more clearly than Senator Stephen A. Douglas. The "Little Giant" of Illinois was already stepping into the large shoes being vacated by the aging champions of national unity, Henry Clay of Kentucky and Lewis Cass of Michigan. Cass, who as governor of Michigan Territory had presided over the upper Mississippi country for 17 years, had visited the river's headwaters, and had left his name on one of its lakes, was the Democratic candidate for president in 1848. During the campaign he addressed the divisive issue of whether slavery would be extended across the continent by advocating local option, or "popular sovereignty." Although Cass's loss to the Whig candidate, Zachary Taylor, was sealed in part by the upstart Free Soilers, whose antislavery platform foreshadowed the tensions that lay ahead, his doctrine of popular sovereignty was adopted by the more charismatic Douglas. The Illinois senator looked to the swelling population of the West along with the powerful forces of economic growth, corporate organization, and outward expansion to counteract the conflict over human slavery.[3]

Like some other western statesmen, Douglas read destiny in the geography of the upper Mississippi region. The river already provided the country with a thousand-mile channel uniting North and South. At the head of steamboat navigation, the tiny hamlet of St. Paul was nourished by a growing commerce that

Senator Stephen A. Douglas of Illinois, who championed the creation of Minnesota Territory

rolled over oxcart trails from the isolated British settlements on the Red River. From there it was not hard to chart the course of American empire across the far-flung private domain of the Hudson's Bay Company to the 54th parallel, where Russian claims began.[4] Moreover, the head of Lake Superior, little more than 100 miles from St. Paul, would eventually give deep-water access to the heart of the continent and be the logical terminus for a transcontinental railroad.

As early as 1846, Douglas, then a congressman, had prevented Iowa from extending its state line north to include the Fort Snelling area and the Falls of St. Anthony. Again in 1847, while Wisconsin struggled toward statehood, he reined in efforts from politicians in Madison to take in St. Paul and the falls by supporting a bill for the organization of "Minasota" Territory. It was tabled, but he revived it again in 1848, for he could see that if the small nucleus of American population growing at the head of river navigation were to be annexed by another state, the remaining northern reaches of the country extending to the British boundary would have little hope of organized government for years to come.[5]

For the time being, economic control on the upper Mississippi lay with a network of traders that was anchored during the 1840s by the firm of Pierre Chouteau Jr. and Company of St. Louis. They included Hercules L. Dousman at Prairie du Chien, his associate, a mercurial newcomer to the Indian trade named Henry M. Rice, and Sibley at Mendota. Formerly Dousman's partner, Sibley by 1846 was working independently with Chouteau, both as trader and land agent. His polish, education, and impeccable social and political connections gave him a recognized claim to leadership. Through a post operated by Norman W. Kittson at Pembina on the British border, he was fast developing a business in buffalo hides from the western plains and smuggled furs from the Hudson's Bay Company preserve.[6]

The late 1840s saw this group alternately challenged and supported by lumbermen moving from Maine and New Hampshire into the rich pine stands of the St. Croix valley, which had been ceded in 1837 by the Ojibwe and Dakota. With financial backing from the northeastern

Those officers were ultimately named by the new president. Chief among them was the governor, Alexander Ramsey, a former Whig congressman from Pennsylvania. Sibley had already been sent to Washington by a quasilegal election held in 1848 and was confirmed as the territory's congressional delegate in August 1849. Legislators, elected at the same time, held their first session at a St. Paul hotel early in September.

WITH THE TERRITORY of 166,000 square miles organized, the prime issues became land and people. A census taken in the summer of 1849 recorded the resident Euro-American population as 4,535. Probably as many as one-third of those were of mixed Indian and European ancestry, including nearly everyone in the widely scattered settlement formed by the descendants of French traders and voyageurs around Pembina. Census takers listed these métis people as white, provided they dressed and lived in European fashion. The Indian population can only be guessed at. Ramsey's estimate was some 25,000—none, of course, considered citizens or voters.

While nearly half the population counted in the census was concentrated in the three towns of St. Paul, Stillwater, and St. Anthony, Indian people were spread widely. On the banks of the Missouri at the far western edge of the territory, more than 400 miles from St. Paul, the Mandan and Hidatsa tribes lived together in an earth-lodge village, Like-a-Fishhook, that was without much question the largest in the territory. Its estimated population of about 700 outnumbered Stillwater and probably surpassed St. Paul.[7]

Not for long, however, was this true. Creation of the new territory turned St. Paul into a feverish little boom town. The population more than doubled within a year, four newspapers appeared, and shanties sprouted like mushrooms along the Mississippi River bluff. Nevertheless, all of the huge territory—except the narrow triangle of land between the St. Croix and the Mississippi Rivers and south of a line running through Lake Mille Lacs—was still Indian country. No treaties of purchase for the rest of the territory had yet been signed. Facing St. Paul across and just down the Mississippi lay the Dakota town of Kaposia, a daily reminder of the fundamental barrier that stood in the way of new immigration.

The human face of that barrier was represented by three tribes: the Dakota or Sioux of southern Minnesota, the Ojibwe or Chippewa to the north, and the Ho-Chunk or Winnebago, who had been moved from their home in central Wisconsin to northern Iowa, promised a place in central Minnesota in 1846, and settled on land bought in 1847 from the Ojibwe. All three

Territorial powers (from right) Henry Sibley, Joseph Rolette Jr. (standing), and unidentified man, possibly Franklin Steele, photographed by Mathew Brady in his Washington, D. C., studio, about 1857

states, these New Englanders began rafting logs down the Mississippi and building sawmills at places like Marine Mills and Stillwater. A personal link between the two groups was Franklin Steele, brother-in-law and business associate of Sibley. Steele owned the key waterpower site at the Falls of St. Anthony, where he built the first sawmill and started producing lumber in September 1848.

Both traders and lumbermen were eager for the jobs, patronage, and wider influence that would accompany a new territory. With the support of Douglas, the Wisconsin boundary was eventually placed at the St. Croix River. Again in 1849 the Illinois senator played a key role at the last moment, saving the bill creating Minnesota Territory from a congressional deadlock over whether the outgoing Democratic or incoming Whig administration would appoint the territorial officers.

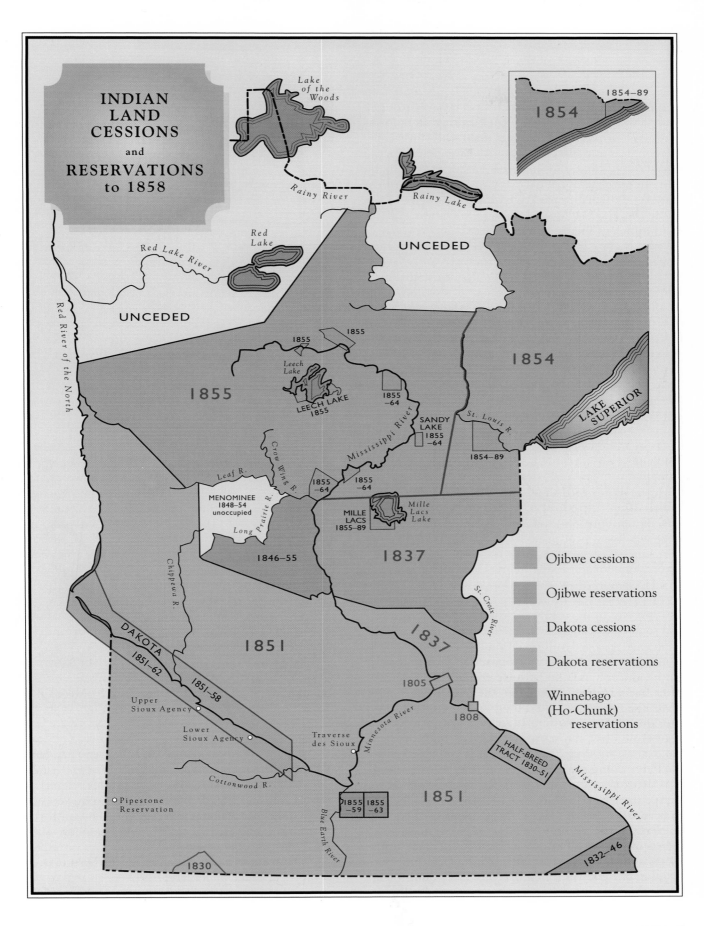

INDIAN
LAND
CESSIONS
and
RESERVATIONS
to 1858

1854

1854–89

Lake
of the
Woods

Rainy River

Rainy Lake

UNCEDED

Red
Lake

Red Lake River

UNCEDED

1855

1855

Leech
Lake

1854

LEECH LAKE
1855

1855
–64

1855
–64

SANDY
LAKE
1855
–64

St. Louis R.

LAKE SUPERIOR

Mississippi River

1854–89

Leaf R.

Crow Wing R.

1855
–64

1855
–64

Mille
Lacs
Lake

MENOMINEE
1848–54
unoccupied

Long Prairie R.

MILLE
LACS
1855–89

Chippewa R.

1846–55

1837

Red River of the North

DAKOTA
1851–62

1851

1837

St. Croix River

1851–58

Upper
Sioux Agency

Lower
Sioux Agency

Traverse
des Sioux

1805

1808

Minnesota River

HALF-BREED
TRACT 1830–51

Mississippi River

Cottonwood R.

Pipestone
Reservation

1855
–59

1855
–63

1851

Blue Earth River

1830

1832–46

Ojibwe cessions

Ojibwe reservations

Dakota cessions

Dakota reservations

Winnebago
(Ho-Chunk)
reservations

groups were acquainted with European ways through traders who had lived and married among them for a century. More recently they had dealt with Christian missionaries and the U.S. Army. All three had experienced the fickleness of the Great Father in Washington and the unreliability of his many agents. Their principal leaders—Little Crow and Wabasha of the Dakota, Hole-in-the-Day and Flat Mouth among the Ojibwe, and Winneshiek of the Ho-Chunk—were canny and wary, yet keenly conscious of the power behind the migrating hordes that were poised to overrun their land.

In his inaugural address to the first legislature, Governor Ramsey targeted purchase of southern Minnesota from the Dakota tribe as the prime need of the new territory. A memorial on the subject was duly sent to Congress, and for the next three years that goal was the central preoccupation of Minnesota citizens. The key to achieving it peacefully was the trading establishment led by Sibley, who had lived and worked for nearly 20 years among the Dakota. Allied with him were powerful mixed-blood families like the Faribaults and Renvilles. Without support from these people and their widespread networks of kin among the four bands of the tribe, there was little hope for getting agreement to a treaty.

It was in July 1851 that Ramsey and Commissioner of Indian Affairs Luke Lea, acting as federal treaty negotiators, met with the Sisseton and Wahpeton bands at Traverse des Sioux, near present-day St. Peter. On the same spot, just 10 years earlier, these Dakota groups had agreed immediately to the treaty that would have created an all-Indian territory. But the Great Father had changed his mind, and in 1851 they were faced with something far different. In the meantime there had been lean years, and some of the people were close to starvation while others had survived only on credit from traders.[8]

The United States now proposed to take all their land as far west as Lake Traverse and the Big Sioux River for its own citizens. When the bargaining was finished, the two bands found themselves confined to a strip of country extending 10 miles on each side of the Minnesota River above the Yellow Medicine River. Below that, another 20-mile-wide strip was reserved for the Mdewakanton and Wahpekute bands, with whom a separate treaty would be made.

For their land they were to be paid about 7.5 cents an acre. Most of the sum would be invested and its interest yield an annuity for 50 years. Some $30,000 was to be spent immediately on schools, mills, blacksmith shops, and other government services, while the remaining $275,000 would be given to the chiefs, who might then pay the debts members of the tribe owed

the traders. This was a feature of nearly every Indian treaty, despite mandates to the contrary often made by Congress in an effort to prevent fraudulent claims. To ensure collection, traders represented at Traverse des Sioux drew up a document listing the debts and secured the signature of each Indian headman as he left the treaty table.

Debate raged later as to whether the Dakota understood the traders' paper, and the procedure gave rise to complaints of fraud and favoritism from other traders.

Those charges led to a congressional investigation that probed the close working relationship between Ramsey and Sibley but found no malfeasance. Most of the small traders who received money as a result of the treaty were deeply in debt to Sibley, who in turn owed nearly all of what he collected to the Chouteau company. Thus, little of the payment stayed in Minnesota.

Meanwhile a separate treaty had been signed at Mendota in August 1851 with the Mdewakanton and Wahpekute. Having already received some treaty money

Dakota leaders lined up to make their signature marks in Francis D. Millet's oil, *The Treaty of Traverse des Sioux,* painted in 1905 from sketches that artist Frank B. Mayer had made at the signing in 1851 from ceding their land east of the Mississippi, the Mdewa-kanton were less hungry and desperate than the others. They were also more determined and suspicious, since they had learned from experience that government payments were always late and that many promises were never kept—facts that Little Crow repeatedly pointed out. But there was nothing they could do except protest. They were trapped by the fact that the western bands had already given in.

LOBBYING THE TREATIES through Congress was again the work of Sibley, this time in his role as territorial delegate. It was a bitter struggle. Southern diehards who opposed national expansion to the north succeeded in amending the documents in a way that they hoped the Indians would reject. One major change was to strike out the provision for a reservation along the Minnesota River and to leave the Dakota with nowhere to go except some unnamed place that the president might designate. The

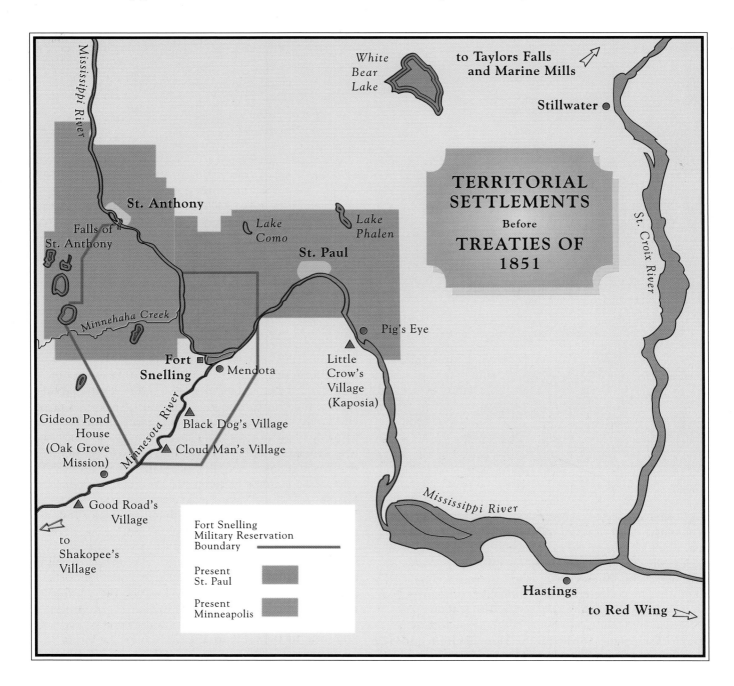

TERRITORIAL SETTLEMENTS Before **TREATIES OF 1851**

Dakota were indeed angered. But Ramsey assured them that the president would name the valley of the Minnesota River as their permanent home, and the revised treaties were reluctantly accepted in the fall of 1852.

During the same years the Indian barrier to the north was also under attack. Ironically, this began with an effort to move more Ojibwe into Minnesota Territory. In 1837 and 1842 they had ceded all of their land in northern Wisconsin, but in both cases treaty negotiators had assured the people that they would not have to move for several generations, if ever. What the United States wanted was only access to timber and minerals. By February, 1850, however, the Great Father had changed his mind, and all of them were told to relocate west of the Mississippi. Governor Ramsey of Minnesota was to take charge of the process.[9]

**Territorial Governor
Alexander Ramsey**

Ramsey planned to put most of them in the neighborhood of Leech Lake, still far from the edge of settlement and away from increasing commerce on Lake Superior. The U.S. Indian agency would be moved from La Pointe, in northern Wisconsin, and the most immediate change he foresaw would be more government business, jobs, and money flowing through St. Paul to northern Minnesota. He took no steps, however, to get agreement from the Ojibwe bands already living around the Mississippi headwaters, and when they objected, the new location was changed to Sandy Lake. Forcing the Wisconsin bands to move was thought to be simple: their annuities, including both money and supplies, would be paid only at Sandy Lake, and any who refused to travel there would receive none.

During the next three years a tangled and tragic tale, marked by incompetence, lies, and callousness to human suffering on the part of both Ramsey and Indian agent John M. Watrous ended in the death of between two and four hundred Ojibwe. They were saved further loss from starvation, exposure, and disease when the election of 1852 sent Democrat Franklin Pierce to the White House. The new administration replaced Ramsey and Watrous with Democratic appointees. Possibly influenced by appeals from the Ojibwe leader Buffalo who with a few others traveled illegally to Washington, the president also cancelled the policy of removal.

Relieved and thankful, the Ojibwe bands around Lake Superior willingly signed a new treaty in 1854. In return for permanent, designated reservations in their own country they gave up the Minnesota Arrowhead, the northeasternmost region of the territory, which was already suspected to contain important mineral wealth. Also included in this treaty was the north bank of the St. Louis River at its mouth, where a sheltered deep-water port provided the key to transportation and commercial expansion at the head of Lake Superior. In 1855 still another section of the barrier against American occupation fell, when the Ojibwe

Little Crow at the Treaty of Traverse des Sioux, an 1895 oil portrait by Frank B. Mayer based on his 1851 sketch

Silver peace medal (reverse side), dated 1853 and presented to Ojibwe chief Hole-in-the-Day II during the administration of President Franklin Pierce

bands around the Mississippi headwaters agreed to a similar arrangement and ceded most of north-central Minnesota. The same year saw the Ho-Chunk again moved, this time to a small reservation in the Blue Earth River valley of southern Minnesota.

WITH THE SIGNING of these treaties a subtle but profound change had already taken place. Prairie and oak openings had become acres; forests had become timber stands; tumbling rivers had become water rights. A world of natural features once invested with mystery and power of their own had become resources for human manipulation. Unlike the Dakota, the Ojibwe had a generation yet ahead of them to accommodate to this transformation. In southern Minnesota, change came more quickly.

To nineteenth-century Americans, too, land had an almost holy quality. The sacred element they saw was not the land itself, with its ancient layers of interwoven plant and animal life, but the dream of what human labor could produce from it. In the words of one anonymous midcentury poet:

The land is the gift of bounteous God,
And to labor his word commands;
Yet millions of hands want acres,
And millions of acres want hands.[10]

Even more alluring and powerful than the natural bounty of land was the meteoric rise in its value as pop-

ulation poured into an area. A tract bought from Indian people for 7.5 cents and resold by the government to its own citizens for $1.25 might be worth hundreds if platted as a town lot or even thousands if it became the business block of a rising city. Successive waves of land speculation built great fortunes and fueled the U.S. economy through much of the nineteenth century, and one of them was cresting just at the time Minnesota became a territory.

Not until February 1853 did the purchase of southern Minnesota from the Dakota become official, and settlement was not legal there until a year and a half later. But the tide would not be held back. As soon as the signing of the treaties was announced late in 1852, a flood of trespassers surged onto Indian land. As at Red Wing in the spring of 1853, the new owners hastened the departure of lingering Dakota neighbors by torching bark houses that stood in their way.

They came on overcrowded steamboats or they walked across Illinois and Wisconsin beside covered wagons—men, women, and children, cattle, pigs, and other livestock. Many were newcomers from Sweden, Germany, Ireland, and other north European countries. Some came as extended families and others accompanied neighbors from the Old Country. Along with their domestic animals they brought seed to replace the native prairie grasses with crops that had fed their ancestors in Europe. Thus, not only the human face but the underlying biological patterns of Minnesota began to change immediately. By 1854 the Euro-American population of the territory was more than 30,000, and just three years later it topped 150,000. Among people over 15 years of age counted in the U.S. census of 1850, white men had outnumbered white women by more than two to one, but by 1860 the ratio was almost one to one.[11]

A sizable number of these people congregated in the new towns that sprang up along the Minnesota and Mississippi Rivers: Carver, Henderson, Mankato, Winona, Wabasha, Read's Landing, Red Wing, Hastings, St. Anthony Falls, and eventually Minneapolis, after the Fort Snelling military reservation was opened to land claims in 1855. The mainstays of this urban frontier were sawmills and river commerce. Farms in the country behind them were still small, producing little more than subsistence crops, and roads to market were few. So throughout the territorial years Minnesota imported food from downriver. Its principal exports remained lumber, hides, and furs.

During these years there was constant agitation for relaxing federal land law, which required that land be surveyed before it could be claimed. In 1854 this was changed for Minnesota to allow pre-emption (registering of a claim) on unsurveyed land. Such claims could be "proved up" later. The great fear of many settlers was that a land auction would be declared before they had the money to buy their claims, and politicians were kept busy working to have such sales postponed. In 1862 the Homestead Act ended this system, but during Minnesota's territorial years grassroots claim associations, which were prepared to defend the rights of vulnerable settlers, were common. So also were scores of "paper towns" platted and promoted in hopes of ballooning land values that were never realized. Along with these came land speculators and loan sharks like Jason C. Easton of Chatfield, who advertised that he made and brokered loans, collected on bad debts, paid taxes, examined titles, and above all located and dealt in military-bounty land warrants. Those certificates for the purchase of government land became a bonanza for speculators after 1855, when Congress gave them as a bonus to Mexican War veterans.[12]

DESPITE GROWING ETHNIC DIVERSITY, the economic, cultural, and political leadership of the territory was held firmly by Anglo-Americans, and the influence of those from northeastern states earned Minnesota the nickname "New England of the West." Laws and institutions embodied that influence. At its first session in 1849, the legislature passed an expansive common-school act, and nine years later 72 school districts offered free education to anyone between the ages of

four and twenty-one. The same legislators chartered a university and proclaimed their keen sense of destiny by creating a historical society. While the university remained a dream for many years, church bodies moved ahead at once to supply the growing need for training schoolteachers and ministers. On the town square of Red Wing in 1856 Hamline University laid stone foundations for the first four-year college west of the Mississippi. The next year it opened its doors, admitting women as well as men. Other than elementary teaching, there was little paid employment for women in the territory, but they undertook social service and nursing when the Sisters of St. Joseph founded St. Paul's first hospital after a cholera epidemic in 1854.[13]

A literate population demanded newspapers, and by 1858 more than 80 had been started in the territory. From their print shops early editors like James M. Goodhue of the *Minnesota Pioneer* and David Olmsted of the *Minnesota Democrat,* both in St. Paul, and Charles G. Ames of the St. Anthony Falls *Minnesota Republican* acted as territorial boosters and opinion makers. In 1857 the first woman's voice was heard, when Jane Grey Swisshelm issued the controversial *St. Cloud Visiter* to champion abolition and women's rights.

IN POLITICS IT WAS A TIME when party lines were shifting all across the nation in response to rising sectional tensions. This was reflected in Minnesota, where parties existed in name only through most of the territorial

Bank note from 1849, a rare surviving example of the territory's fledgling economy

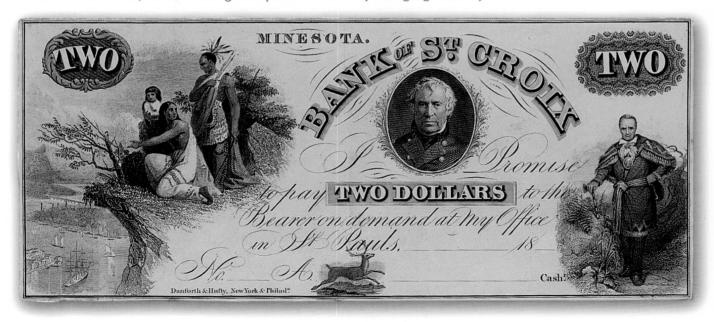

years. Although replaced as governor by Democrat Willis A. Gorman in 1853, Ramsey remained a power, far outweighing the influence of the few other local Whigs. As his party began to disintegrate he played a waiting game, refusing to commit to the new Minnesota Republican Party, organized in 1855, until it gained unmistakable momentum. Sibley, a moderate Democrat, had strong personal and political ties to Cass and Douglas but, following the nonpartisan model set by Cass in Michigan Territory, he maintained local allies in all camps. Sibley's chief rival, Henry M. Rice, with whom he had quarreled in business and continued to quarrel in politics, was nonpartisan in his own way. As the national Democratic Party threatened to split between northern and southern wings, Rice, a skilled lobbyist and office-seeker, remained a friend of whoever was in power. With unfailing charm and cheerful cynicism, he brought the spoils from Washington back to Minnesota.

A year after Minnesota emerged as a political entity, Cass, from his position as senior statesman and senator from Michigan, stitched together the patchwork of agreements known as the Compromise of 1850. It was

Desk set used in the 1856 territorial legislature by Representative Thomas W. Pierce of Richfield, Hennepin County: wax sealer with wooden handle, maple sand shaker (for blotting), and cast-iron paperweight

made possible by the pressure of economic interests from both North and South. With an immediate confrontation over slavery postponed, Douglas and others turned to an emerging network of corporate enterprise that they hoped would support a political coalition powerful enough to hold the nation back from war.

This new force rode on the steel rails that were even then transforming the country by shrinking time and distance. Douglas himself had performed a political coup in 1850 when he secured to the state of Illinois the first major grant of federal land for purposes of railroad building. He envisioned an expanding web, knitting the country together, with the Illinois Central system at its heart. Southern extensions would reach into Texas, and its northern anchor would be a new city named Superior at the head of the big lake.[14]

That city, platted in 1853 on the Wisconsin side of the St. Louis River, further expressed the continental dreams that had gone into the making of Minnesota Territory. A possible route for a transcontinental railroad west from Lake Superior was even then being explored by the U.S. Army. The Sault Canal, already under construction, would bring shipping from the lower lakes to the head of Lake Superior within two years. But the most immediate step would be building a rail line that would link the lake with St. Paul and extend on through Minnesota and Iowa where it would connect with a branch of the Illinois Central.

Then, as now, money ruled politics. In accord with Douglas's vision, shares in the far northern boom town were distributed to a host of influential Democratic politicians from both the southern and northern wings of the party, while much of the capital for its development came from the deep pockets of William W. Corcoran, a Washington-based financier with strong southern sympathies. In Minnesota, where the charter and a land grant for the proposed railroad link had to originate, all political factions were brought to the table, including Sibley, Ramsey, Gorman, and others less prominent. Henry Rice was among the first and most closely involved. After trying to make his own claims on the site of the town of Superior, he had come to terms with the agents of Douglas and was actively promoting the railroad scheme.

Rice had succeeded Sibley as Minnesota's territorial delegate in 1853, and a temporary truce prevailed between them. Then, early in 1854, lobbyists from the Illinois Central company strong-armed the territorial legislature into passing the charter of the new Minnesota and North

Western Railroad Company, with a provision that any land grant made to Minnesota for railroad building would automatically go to that company. Sibley became increasingly cool, and Congress also proved skittish about such a restrictive arrangement. One land-grant bill introduced by Rice was defeated.

As the price of his support for a second attempt, Sibley demanded the right to draw up the bill himself. In doing so, he worded it carefully so that the Minnesota and North Western would not be eligible to receive the grant. That version was successful in Congress, but jubilation in Minnesota came to a screeching halt when it was found that the law's wording had been altered to favor the company some time between its passage by the House of Representatives and its signing by the president. The resulting scandal sunk both the land grant and the Minnesota and North Western.

Thus, the steel rails that might have stretched from St. Paul to Superior in 1855 were not laid until 1870, and the whole railroad era in Minnesota was delayed beyond the end of the territorial years. Although Minnesota's isolation during the months when the Mississippi was frozen had been partially overcome by government roads and stagecoach lines established in the territorial years, the need for all-weather transportation remained, and the political scheming and burning desire for a share in the economic bonanza promised by railroads played an important role in the rush toward statehood.

TIME WAS RUNNING OUT for the promoters of Superior and the Illinois Central, for in 1857 the wave of prosperity that had supported the northwest region's phenomenal growth crashed on the rocks of financial panic. Money became tight throughout the country and almost nonexistent in Minnesota; land values collapsed, and western settlement slowed. Superior shrank into a frontier outpost, and even exuberant St. Paul was thrown into the doldrums for several years.

For the political vision of Illinois's Little Giant, time had also run out. Far from defusing the slavery issue, the doctrine of popular sovereignty, embodied in the Kansas-Nebraska Act of 1854, had brought outright warfare to the territory of Kansas. The forces of corporate empire-building and interlocking material interests had not proved strong enough to contain those of moral outrage and cultural conflict. Thus, when Minnesota delegates gathered in the summer of 1857 to draw up a state constitution, the shadow of "Bleeding Kansas" hung over them. The flaming issues that divided them were the status of black people, both free and slave, and the new relationships implied by a recent decision of the U.S. Supreme Court, which held that Harriet and

Territorial delegate to Congress Henry M. Rice

Thirty-hour shelf clock, made in Connecticut by
E. N. Welch Manufacturing Company and brought to
Minnesota Territory by Gottfried Henneberg

1650s–70s
• European explorers encounter
Ojibwe and Dakota inhabitants of
Minnesota region

1787
• Some Ojibwe and Dakota lands
included in Northwest Territory of
the U.S.

1803
• Louisiana Purchase acquires for the
U.S. 828,000 square miles of Indian-
occupied land between Mississippi
River and Rocky Mountains

1805–06
• Zebulon M. Pike, an American
army officer, explores parts of
Minnesota region

1812
• Red River colony (Winnipeg)
started by Lord Selkirk, a Scottish
nobleman

1818
• Convention with Great Britain
establishes 49th parallel as northern
boundary of the U.S. from Lake of
the Woods to Rocky Mountains

1819
• Fort Snelling established as north-
westernmost army post on the U.S.
frontier

1820s
• American fur trade peaks in
Minnesota

1820
• Missouri compromise bans slavery
in Louisiana Territory north of
36°30′ (southern boundary of
Missouri)

1823
• First mail-carrying steamboat, based
at St. Louis, reaches Fort Snelling

1834
• Missionaries arrive in Minnesota to convert Indians to Christianity

1836
• Slave Dred Scott brought to Fort Snelling by his owner, an army surgeon

1837
• First major treaties with Ojibwe and Dakota take east-central Minnesota and adjacent Wisconsin for white settlement

1839
• Pierre Parrant constructs shanty at "Pig's Eye" (St. Paul)

1846
• Iowa admitted as 29th state Mexican-American War begins

1847
• Harriet Bishop starts Minnesota's first school in St. Paul

1848
• Gold discovered in California
• U.S. acquires California, the Southwest, and Rio Grande boundary area at end of war with Mexico
• Wisconsin admitted as 30th state, leaving Minnesota area without government
• Mass northern European migration to U.S. begins
• Stillwater Convention stimulates Minnesota's drive for territorial status

1849
• Minnesota Territory organized with less than 5,000 people
• First newspapers in Minnesota published

1850
• Compromise of 1850 calms slavery controversy by permitting California to enter Union as a nonslave state, opening Utah and New Mexico Territories to slavery at statehood, prohibiting slave trade in District of Columbia, and increasing power of slave owners to retrieve runaway slaves
• First U.S. census in Minnesota shows population of 6,077

1851
• 200,000 Irish emigrate to U.S. to escape potato famine
• By treaties of Mendota and Traverse des Sioux, the Dakota cede their land west of Mississippi River (southern and western Minnesota) to the U.S.
• St. Paul, St. Anthony (merged with Minneapolis in 1872), and Stillwater selected as sites of capital, university, and penitentiary
• Caravan of 102 Red River oxcarts arrives in St. Paul

1852
• *Grammar and Dictionary of the Dakota Language,* compiled by Stephen R. Riggs, Thomas S. Williamson, and Gideon and Samuel Pond, published by Smithsonian Institution

1854
• Kansas-Nebraska Act reopens slavery controversy by repealing the Missouri Compromise and allowing voters to decide the status of slavery in the two territories
• By Treaty of La Pointe, the Ojibwe cede northeastern Minnesota to the U.S.
• U.S. legalizes pre-emption, granting purchase rights to the first claimant on unsurveyed land in Minnesota and Iowa
• Rock Island Railroad excursion brings tourists and publicity to Minnesota

1855
• Mississippi, Pillager, and Winnibigoshish bands of Ojibwe cede their lands in central and northern Minnesota to the U.S.
• Minnesota's Republican Party organized in response to formation of national party in 1854
• First bridge to span Mississippi River's main channel anywhere along its length opens between Minneapolis and St. Anthony

1857
• National financial panic ends prosperity that has supported Minnesota Territory's growth
• U.S. Supreme Court exacerbates slavery controversy by ruling in Dred Scott case that Scott's residency in Minnesota Territory did not entitle him to sue for freedom
• Pre-statehood census shows territorial population of 150,037
• Democrats and Republicans hold rival constitutional conventions in anticipation of statehood
• Attempt to remove Minnesota's capital to St. Peter

1858
• Trans-Atlantic cable connecting U.S. and England laid
• Minnesota admitted as 32nd state

1859
• Oregon admitted as 33rd state

1860
• Abraham Lincoln elected president Southern states begin seceding

1861
• Governor Alexander Ramsey pledges President Lincoln 1,000 volunteers, making Minnesota the first state to offer troops to the Union cause

Dred Scott were still slaves, although they had lived for years at Fort Snelling in free territory. So hot were tempers that Minnesota's Democrats and Republicans met separately and drew up different constitutions.

Local self-interest remained alive and well, nevertheless. Statehood promised not only influence in debates at the national level but control over local borrowing and taxation. A crucial incentive was the continuing fever to subsidize and promote railroads, including the prospect of a transcontinental line running through Minnesota to the Pacific. Compromise was therefore reached outside the meeting rooms, and a single constitution was at last agreed upon.

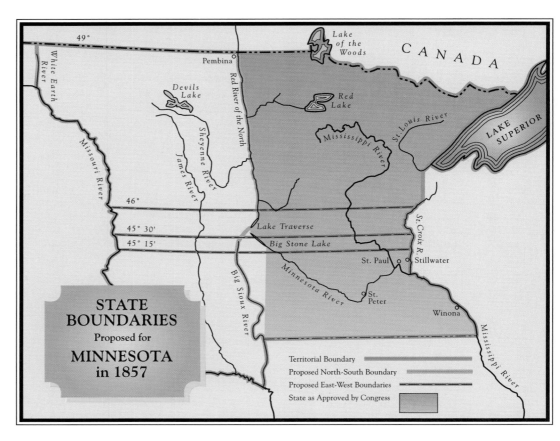

STATE
BOUNDARIES
Proposed for
MINNESOTA
in 1857

Territorial Boundary
Proposed North-South Boundary
Proposed East-West Boundaries
State as Approved by Congress

In anticipation of statehood, elections were held that pitted Sibley, who campaigned as an antislavery Democrat, in a race for governor against Ramsey, the new champion of Minnesota Republicans. Margins were narrow but Sibley prevailed, and Democrats won most of the offices. The elected legislators agreed to send Henry Rice to the U.S. Senate. Candidates for the other Senate seat were deadlocked, and the choice went to a dark horse named James Shields, a former Illinois senator and friend of Douglas. With Congress immobilized over Kansas, Minnesota's admission was held up for months, but at last, on May 11, 1858, the territory became a state.

Its shape had been hotly debated. Some had argued that Minnesota should extend west to the Missouri and north only to the 46th parallel (the latitude of present-day Little Falls). Less compelling alternatives set the northern boundary at 45°30′, 45°15′, or even farther south. Such a state would have included most of Minnesota's immigrant farmers and a majority of Republican voters. The influence of Democrats Rice and

Douglas in Washington, however, had ensured that an elongated north-south shape was specified in the enabling act passed by Congress, and this ultimately prevailed. In reaching to the British line and including the envisioned railroad route from Lake Superior westward, it reflected the continuing strength of expansionist ambitions.

As early as 1851 Ramsey had ridden to Pembina to negotiate with the Ojibwe a treaty of purchase for part of the Red River Valley. Congress had failed to ratify it, but throughout the territorial years trade with the British colony to the north had steadily increased. The first three years of statehood saw an even stronger push in that direction, with the building of a stage and wagon road to supplement the meandering oxcart trails that had served since the 1830s. A move was also made to open steamboat navigation on the Red River. These efforts were temporarily suspended, however, by the Civil and Dakota wars.[15]

In the interval thus created, Britain began the slow process of consolidating civil government in its sprawling North American territories and reached out to establish control over the Red River settlement and the restive *gens libres,* or métis, of the northern plains. With this, the vision of American territorial expansion began to fade, although in Minnesota it flickered a short time longer, encouraged by the U.S. purchase of Alaska in 1867 and the Riel Rebellion of 1870 in Manitoba. But although the 49th parallel remained the international line, bioregions, human communities, and economic interests continued to ignore it. Before the first railroad was opened from Minnesota to Puget Sound, Canadian citizen James J. Hill's St. Paul, Minneapolis, and Manitoba Railroad, financed by the Bank of Montreal, was carrying grain from Manitoba to the mills of Minneapolis.

THE NINE TERRITORIAL YEARS had set the stage for transforming the natural and cultural landscapes of the upper Mississippi country into those of a "civilized" Euro-American community. The undisturbed systems of plant and animal life that Americans called "wilderness" were converted into commodities subject to ownership and exchange. A way of life that regarded them as eternal and necessary for human existence was ruthlessly eliminated. As a result, the scene was also prepared for the tragic drama that drenched Minnesota's western prairies in blood when the Dakota made a last desperate effort to take back their country in 1862.

Still in the future during the territorial years was the time when the forests would be slashed and the curves of prairie land would be regimented into rectangular fields fenced with barbed wire and deeds. Even farther in the future was the time when Minnesota could boast of being the world's breadbasket and its iron mines would build the steel infrastructure of an industrial society. And undreamed-of yet was the swelling metropolitan area that would leap even state lines to become the transportation, economic, and cultural hub of the whole region between the upper Great Lakes and the Rocky Mountains. The script, however, was already in place. 🐎

NOTES

[1] Unless otherwise noted, factual material for this article can be found in standard sources on Minnesota history, especially volume 1 of William W. Folwell's *A History of Minnesota* (St. Paul: Minnesota Historical Society, 1956) and Theodore C. Blegen, *Minnesota: A History of the State* (Minneapolis: University of Minnesota Press, 1963).

[2] For an account of this treaty, negotiated by Wisconsin Governor James D. Doty, see Rhoda R. Gilman, "A Northwestern Indian Territory—The Last Voice," paper delivered at the annual meeting of the Western History Association, Oct. 1997, forthcoming in *Journal of the West.*

[3] The most recent biography of Cass emphasizes his role as a negotiator and compromiser; see Willard C. Klunder, *Lewis Cass and the Politics of Moderation* (Kent, Oh.: Kent State University Press, 1996). On Douglas, see Robert W. Johannsen, *Stephen A. Douglas* (New York: Oxford University Press, 1973).

[4] The southern limit of Russian claims was 54°40′. As early as the election of 1844, Polk's supporters had coined the campaign slogan "54-40 or Fight," but destiny soon manifested to the south, and the U.S. and Great Britain compromised to set the northern border of Oregon at the 49th parallel.

[5] For a full discussion of the controversy over the Wisconsin state boundary and the creation of Minnesota Territory, see William E. Lass, "Minnesota's Separation from Wisconsin: Boundary Making on the Upper Mississippi Frontier," *Minnesota History* 50 (Winter 1987): 309–20, and "The Birth of Minnesota," *Minnesota History* 55 (Summer 1997): 267–79.

[6] Rhoda R. Gilman, "Last Days of the Upper Mississippi Fur Trade," *Minnesota History* 42 (Winter 1970): 122–40.

[7] Folwell, *History of Minnesota,* 1: 351–52; Roy W. Meyer, *The Village Indians of the Upper Missouri: The Mandans, Hidatsas, and Arikaras* (Lincoln: University of Nebraska Press, 1977), 104.

[8] For full accounts of the 1851 treaty, see Folwell, *History of Minnesota,* 1: 266–304; Lucile M. Kane, "The Sioux Treaties and the Traders," *Minnesota History* 32 (June 1951): 65–80.

[9] On the Ojibwe removal effort, see James A. Clifton, "Wisconsin Death March: Explaining the Extremes in the Old Northwest Indian Removal," *Transactions of the Wisconsin Academy of Sciences. Arts and Letters* 75 (1987): 1–39; Ronald N. Satz, "Chippewa Treaty Rights: The Reserved Rights of Wisconsin's Chippewa Indians in Historical Perspective," *Transactions of the Wisconsin Academy of Sciences, Arts and Letters* 79 (1991): 51–59.

[10] "The Acres and the Hands," *Daily Minnesotian* (St. Paul), Dec. 18, 1860.

[11] See United States Historical Census Data Browser, with data from 1790 to 1970, http://fisher.lib.virginia.edu/census/.

[12] Rodney C. Loehr, "Jason C. Easton, Territorial Banker," *Minnesota History* 29 (Sept. 1948): 223–30.

[13] Sister Helen Angela Hurley, "The Sisters of St. Joseph and the Minnesota Frontier," *Minnesota History* 30 (Mar. 1949): 9.

[14] For development of Superior and the political dreams and railroad schemes surrounding it, see Henry Cohen, *Business and Politics in America from the Age of Jackson to the Civil War: The Career Biography of W. W. Corcoran* (Westport, Conn.: Greenwood Press, 1971), 159–201. See also Johannsen, *Douglas,* 304–21, 435–37.

[15] See Rhoda R. Gilman, Carolyn Gilman, and Deborah M. Stultz, *The Red River Trails: Oxcart Routes Between St. Paul and the Selkirk Settlement 1820–1870* (St. Paul: Minnesota Historical Society, 1979).

A DAY IN THE LIFE *of*
Ojibwe

ONE WINTER DAY late in 1850, Ojibwe thought back over the year that was ending. He was 30 years old. Both he and his tribe shared the same name, a point of pride for the young man. Ojibwe was neither a civil nor a war chief. He was not a spiritual leader. However, like many of his people, he was, through circumstance and birth, directly and inextricably linked to the huge shifts and changes affecting his community. His father, Zoongakamig (Strong Ground), and uncle Bagone-giizhig (Hole-in-the-Day I) had been defending Ojibwe lands and livelihoods from the Dakota Indians and American intruders since the early 1800s, and 1850 was a time of great change.[1]

In the fall of that year Ojibwe had traveled to Crow Wing with other members of his band and family to winter where they could hunt for food and trap beaver and muskrat to sell for supplies. They had harvested, parched, jigged, and stored wild rice in pitch-lined birchbark containers near the portages and trails they used during the winter, as their people had been doing for centuries. Ojibwe saw the ducks beginning to migrate, but a mallard or wood duck would have been a delicacy, a rare treat, for him. Ojibwe didn't have a shotgun, and those who did saved their ammunition for bigger game or kept it in reserve in case there was any trouble with Dakota warriors.

When he arrived at Crow Wing he

Daguerreotype of Ojibwe's cousin Bagone-giizhig (Hole-in-the-Day) II, 1855

saw that hundreds of other Ojibwe people had already gathered. Crow Wing always became densely populated at that season. A winter hunting site for Ojibwe living at Sandy Lake, Mille Lacs, and Leech Lake since the early 1800s, it had become a true, rugged border town after the 1847 Ojibwe treaty ceded the region. White traders had flooded in to take advantage of the new Ho-chunk (Winnebago) and Menominee reservations as well as the older Ojibwe communities. By 1850 Crow Wing had a substantial white population as well as a growing and powerful mixed-blood trading elite. Liquor

was a staple trade item, and gambling was as common as trade.[2]

Warfare was taboo in the colder months when Ojibwe and his family focused their energies on hunting, fishing, and trapping. If men had been diverted to war, the people would have starved to death. Therefore, both the Ojibwe and Dakota people traveled to the border regions in the winter and often lived, hunted, and fished together. The Ojibwe called this practice *biindigodaadiwin*— to enter one another's lodges.[3]

The winter before this, Ojibwe and his cousin Bagone-giizhig II had visited and hunted with the Dakota at Crow Wing. Then, in spring, they went on a daring raid to the heart of Dakota territory around St. Paul with only two other companions. After traveling by canoe for more than 80 miles, they ambushed a lone Dakota man. Ojibwe shot and scalped him, then quickly retreated across the river, being chased all the while by nearby Dakota warriors.[4] Now, Ojibwe gambled and told stories with his Dakota friends in the evening. He and his sometimes enemies knew that after winter was over they would return to their summer villages and perhaps fight each other.

Such alliances weren't normal for Ojibwe or his band, but he was living in trying times. In 1850 the reservation system was beginning to put an end to older life cycles and challenge his entire culture. Ojibwe, his friends and family, and his Dakota counterparts were all profoundly affected by the vast changes taking place.

Like many natives, Ojibwe's growing-up years had been filled with tragedy. Both of his brothers and his mother had been killed by Dakota warriors. And, like many others, Ojibwe's father, Strong Ground, had died of alcohol poisoning in 1845. His uncle, Bagone-giizhig I, had fallen out of an oxcart in a drunken stupor after treaty negotiations with the Americans in 1847 and had been crushed to death.[5]

By 1850, when the creation of Minnesota Territory was being lauded as one of the greatest advancements of civilization in the region, Ojibwe and his people were feeling more pressure on their lands, livelihoods, and lives than ever before. The fur trade that had enabled them to sustain and even increase their standard of living during the period of French explorations was declining. In order to keep his children well fed, Ojibwe, like other Indian people, had to use every resource at his disposal.

While the Ojibwe and Dakota had a complex and sometimes bizarre relationship, nothing was as strange as their newest neighbors, the Americans. When Americans began to talk of land cessions, Ojibwe found the concept hard to fathom. He and many other young Indians didn't trust the American officials, but times were hard. Game was increasingly scarce, and even their children went hungry. When the Americans promised annual payments of food and money in return for land cessions, Ojibwe and others in his community said no. But when the Americans said that the Indians could still

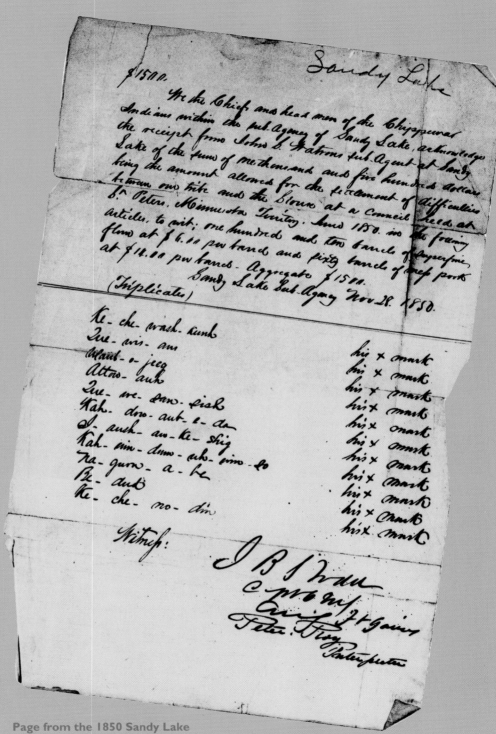

Page from the 1850 Sandy Lake annuity-payment rolls, acknowledging receipt of superfine flour and pork valued at $1,500

hunt and fish on that land, Ojibwe and many companions acquiesced.

Ojibwe felt trapped by the new treaties. He needed the money and food annuities to support his family, but he had never depended on anyone for that before. He was even more frustrated when white people streamed into the ceded lands and, in clear violation of the treaties, stopped him from hunting there. White traders offered Ojibwe food on credit, but when the next treaty signing came they used those claims to take most of his annuity payments. Trapped like the otter he harvested every winter, Ojibwe had to sign more treaties to get more annuities. The more he gave up, the harder it became to live as he and his ancestors had for centuries.

And just when Ojibwe thought things couldn't get any worse, they did. In the fall of 1850 he and his cousin, the young chief Hole-in-the-Day II, along with some 3,000 Ojibwe people had gone to Sandy Lake to receive their annuity payments. The invigorating feeling of being party to such a large gathering quickly turned to horror, however. American officials fed the Indians spoiled meat. As many as 400 people died from food poisoning and dysentery. Ojibwe, Hole-in-the-Day II, and other Indians felt that the poisoning was intentional. American officials claimed it was an accident, however, and no reparations were made.[6]

Ojibwe had always been proud of his warrior traditions. The Dakota scalp he took in the spring of 1850 was not his first. Yet, more than his skills as a fighter, he was proudest of his self-sufficiency, his ability to feed his family and live well by the work of his own hands—hunting, trapping, and fishing. He loved the land—the pristine lakes and huge stands of white and red pine. As much as anybody ever could, he owned that land

and knew it intimately. Now he was being forced off of it, and his skills as a woodsman had no testing ground. Ojibwe was faced with a gut-wrenching decision and the ultimate test of his character and resourcefulness. How would he meet that attack? Would he run and seek refuge in alcohol? Would he try to adapt to the ways of the white man for everything from religion to economy? Would he cling ever stronger to the ways of his prayerful people and fight the onslaught by refusing to give in? The dilemma that Ojibwe faced on that December day in 1850 was that of all Ojibwe people.

OJIBWE STOOD FIRM *for everything he valued—to protect his family, his people, and their shared culture. He survived that way through Minnesota statehood, the U.S.-Dakota conflict in 1862, and removal to a new reservation at White Earth in the late 1860s. He was alive to hear about the Battle of the Little Big Horn. He lived to witness the advent of electricity, the telephone, and the first radio transmission in 1906, although he never acquired any of these luxuries in his own home. He outlived Queen Victoria, who died in 1901. At the ripe age of 91, Ojibwe passed away at his home on White Earth Indian Reservation in 1911.[7]*

Many of his tribesmen were not so resilient. They succumbed to the bullets and diseases brought by the invaders. Or they took their own lives slowly through vicious drinking. While many perished in the assault on their lives and livelihoods, Ojibwe and people like him survived to tell their stories and build a new future for their families and all who came after. Resiliency and survival, even more than tragedy and change, are the legacy of Ojibwe's life and times.

—Anton Treuer and David Treuer

NOTES

[1] Ojibwe (1820–1911) was the son of Strong Ground, a leader from Sandy Lake who had helped establish a new village around Gull Lake. William W. Warren, *History of the Ojibway People* (1885; reprint, St. Paul: Minnesota Historical Society [MHS] Press, 1984), 47; Mark Diedrich, *The Chiefs Hole-in-the-Day of the Mississippi Chippewa* (Minneapolis: Coyote Books, 1986), 14.

[2] Crow Wing became a populous, permanent Ojibwe settlement under the leadership of Ojibwe's cousin, Hole-in-the-Day II; Diedrich, *Chiefs Hole-in-the-Day*, 13; Julia A. Spears, "Reminiscence of Hole-in-the-Day," 2, Julia A. Spears and Family Papers, MHS. On the treaty, see William W. Folwell, *A History of Minnesota* (St. Paul: MHS, 1956), 1:310, 324.

[3] Warren, *History of the Ojibway*, 267.

[4] Diedrich, *Chiefs Hole-in-the-Day*, 21.

[5] Diedrich, *Chiefs Hole-in-the-Day*, 14–15. See also, Stephen R. Riggs, *Tah-Koo Wah-Kan: The Gospel Among the Dakotas* (Boston: Congregational Sabbath School and Publishing Society, 1869), 444; Mary Eastman, *Dahcotah: Or, the Life and Legends of the Sioux* (1849; reprint, Minneapolis: Ross and Haines, 1962), 205. Bagone-giizhig's death was widely reported in local newspapers.

[6] *Minnesota Democrat* (St. Paul), Jan. 21, 1851; Helen H. Tanner, ed., *Atlas of Great Lakes Indian History* (Norman: University of Oklahoma Press, 1987), 167; Diedrich, *Chiefs Hole-in-the-Day*, 21–22.

[7] Ojibwe was active in affairs at White Earth, even in his later years. See Melissa Meyer, *The White Earth Tragedy: Ethnicity and Dispossession at a Minnesota Anishinaabe Reservation, 1889–1920* (Lincoln: University of Nebraska Press, 1994), 105.

A DAY IN THE LIFE *of*

The *Gens Libres*

ON THE UPPER REACHES of the Sheyenne River, the pastel dawn outlined a flat horizon, a geometric line parting the elements of grass and sky. On July 4, 1850, the gray light picked out the camp of the *gens libres*—the freemen—lying on a grassy plateau above the wooded river course. They were the people of the country, the *bois brulé* descendants of European fur traders and their Indian wives. "What a gipsy-like class they are," wrote a Hudson's Bay Company man. "They cordially detest all the laws and restraints of civilized life, believing all men were born to be free."[1]

Their camp was the size of a traveling town, holding 620 hunters, 650 women, 360 children, 542 dogs, 1,058 horses, and 586 oxen. The walls of the town (for they were in the territory of their enemies, the Dakota) were formed by 1,210 two-wheeled carts, or *charettes*, parked side by side in a huge circle with their wooden shafts pointing out. Inside the circle, the peoples' tents of buffalo hide and canvas were pitched at one end; at the other, the horses were corralled. A buffalo runner fetched from $100 to $300, so no one took a chance on his horse straying or getting stolen.[2]

They had set out from the village of Pembina on the Red River on June 21, having gathered there from scattered settlements on both sides of the international boundary in order to follow the chase. Some of them were second- and third-generation buffalo hunters, for brigades had been assembling twice a year—June and September—since about 1820. At Pembina they had elected officers and decided on the rules of the hunt. There were 10 captains—each with 10 soldiers under him—to act as policemen, prevent parties from straying off, and keep order in the

Family of *gens libres* preparing a meal in camp, 1858

Canadian artist Paul Kane's oil painting, *Half Breeds Running Buffalo*, about 1846

camp. The captains took turns acting as guide or chief of the expedition, one per day.[3]

At the first light, a horn roused the sleepers. The homemade flag of the *gens libres* nation went up, and soon all the camp was astir—the women striking the tents, the men harnessing the oxen and horses. They did not pause for breakfast, and there was little to eat, anyway. They had been searching for buffalo in vain but had great hopes this day, since the evening before the scouts had spotted fresh dung. They had all fallen asleep to the eerie music of wolves—always a sure sign that buffalo were near.

Within half an hour, the train was in motion. It was a creaking, snakelike procession, five or six miles long. The women drove the carts, perched atop heaps of baggage, dressed in calico or bright tartan plaid. Wild, wolfish dogs ran in and out among the vehicles, and troops of loose horses pranced alongside. The men, mounted on their showiest steeds, were mostly dressed in blue *capotes*, or hooded coats, generously studded with shiny brass buttons. Their pants were of corduroy or moleskin, their shirts of checked flannel, and on their heads were jaunty Scotch caps. Their tasseled red sashes were a kind of ethnic

badge, as were their brightly beaded or quill-worked moccasins. The people themselves were of all colors, from "the ruddy cheek and blue eyes of the fair-haired Gael" to the bronzed skin and "long masses of straight black hair" inherited from Indian ancestors. Their hubbub of shouts and banter combined French, Gaelic, English, Cree, Ojibwe, and their own evolving language, "a provincial jargon of French and Indian mixed up together," known today as *mitchif*.[4]

Shortly before noon, just as the leader was sounding the horn, the signal for stragglers to catch up, a rider appeared, galloping down the near side of a ridge. Everyone knew what it meant: buffalo were near. Quickly, the hunters rushed to saddle up their buffalo runners. The horses knew what was in the wind and stood shivering with excitement, snuffing the air. By the time the messenger arrived, 400 huntsmen were mounted and ready to ride at the captain's word.[5]

They rode as far as the ridge, then paused while the captain crept forward to survey the herd with his spyglass. Seeing that the buffalo were headed toward rocky ground riddled with prairie-dog holes, he ordered a group to circle around and head them off toward level prairie. The main body of hunters waited behind the ridge, watching as the massive, bearded bulls who led the herd drew closer to the outriders, the animals' poor eyesight preventing them from sensing danger until they smelled the horses; then, they turned in their tracks. At that moment, the hunters erupted over the ridge in full pursuit.

The sound of the horses' hooves was like a volley of artillery, but when the thousand buffalo began to run it was like the shock of an earthquake. Dust rose from the dry ground, darkening the air, and the smell of musk from the bulls was heavy. The grass crackled under their hooves, as if it were on fire. At first, the buffaloes could keep ahead of the horses, but they soon tired, and then the hunters were in the midst of the herd.

They picked out the fat cows first since they had the tenderest meat. Guns went off in volleys. Their flintlock Northwest trade guns fired only one shot at a time. A hunter reloaded at a gallop, drawing the plug of his powder flask with his teeth, pouring in a hasty charge, settling it with a sharp blow against the saddle, spitting a wet bullet from his mouth into the barrel, then holding the gun upright until the moment came to

fire. He trusted his horse to keep clear of the slashing horns and to jump away after a shot to avoid being crushed by the falling body. The muzzle of the gun had to be close enough to graze the monster's shaggy side in order to have any effect.

The melee continued for an hour or more—shots to right and left, horses stumbling, riders falling, dead and wounded animals tumbling over, all in a haze of gunpowder and dust. Then, one after another of the hunters drew rein, dismounted from their drenched horses, and walked back through the heaps of dead buffalo and the puddles of blood, singling out of the hundreds slain the ones that they had shot. They seldom argued or forgot which ones belonged to them.

Over the hill the carts came, driven by the women, and the work of butchering began. Though they *could* use virtually every part of the buffalo, they *did* use very little of most carcasses—sometimes only the tongue and liver, while the rest was left to rot. They took as many skins as the women could reasonably hope to cure. Buffalo hides fetched good prices at faraway St. Paul, but getting them there unspoiled was a challenge.

Abundance reigned in the camp that evening. As the people feasted around their campfires, the fiddle and bagpipe wailed, and old men told stories of buffalo hunts gone by. Before the light died out of the western sky, everyone was wrapped in blankets or robes, the sweet smell of kinnickinnic from their pipes lingering in the air, and the only sound was the exultant howling of the wolves, feasting on the remains of the hunt.[6]

"There is no earthly consideration would make them relinquish the pursuit," wrote one visitor to the land of the *gens libres*, "so fascinating is the sweet air of freedom."[7]

—*Carolyn Gilman*

NOTES

[1] This 1850 story is based on two nearly identical accounts of buffalo hunts from 1840 and 1859: Alexander Ross, *The Red River Settlement: Its Rise, Progress, and Present State* (1856; reprint, Minneapolis: Ross and Haines, 1957), quote, 242, 252; and Manton Marble, "To Red River and Beyond," *Harper's New Monthly Magazine*, Oct. 1860, p. 587–89. Another account, from 1846, appears in Paul Kane, *Wanderings of an Artist among the Indians of North America* (1859), reprinted in J. Russell, *Paul Kane's Frontier* (Austin: University of Texas Press, 1971), 69–72.

[2] The population figures are for the hunt of 1840; the numbers in 1850 may have been larger. Ross, *Red River Settlement,* 244, 246. For the price of buffalo runners, see Marble, "To Red River and Beyond," *Harper's,* Oct. 1860, p. 586.

[3] Ross, *Red River Settlement,* 245–50.

[4] Ross, *Red River Settlement,* 190–91, 200 (quote), 248, 250; Marble, "To Red River and Beyond," *Harper's,* Aug. 1860, p. 305, Oct. 1860, p. 588; James Carnegie, Earl of Southesk, *Saskatchewan and the Rocky Mountains* (Edinburgh: Edmonston and Douglas, 1875), 44 (quote), 45; "The People of the Red River," *Harper's,* Jan. 1859, p. 169–70 (quote); Charles Hallock, "The Red River Trail," *Harper's,* Apr. 1859, p. 615.

[5] Here and four paragraphs below, see Marble, "To Red River," *Harper's,* Oct. 1860, p. 588–89; Ross, *Red River Settlement,* 255–57, 261; "People of the Red River," *Harper's,* Jan. 1859, p. 176; William H. Keating, *Narrative of an Expedition to the Source of St. Peter's River* (London: George B. Whittaker, 1825), 2:27.

[6] Marble, "To Red River," *Harper's,* Oct. 1860, p. 588.

[7] Ross, *Red River Settlement,* 243, 260.

BRUCE M. WHITE

The Power of Whit

eness

I N MARCH 1857 A SHORT, merry, prank-loving member of the
Minnesota territorial legislature made away with a recently passed
bill in order to prevent it from going into law. For several days he stayed
holed up in a local hotel where he ate sumptuous meals, drank fine wines
and whiskies, played poker, and partied with his male and female friends.
On the last day of the legislative session, just as the final gavel fell, he
appeared, ready to report the bill, to the laughter of supporters and
opponents alike. The following day he was paraded by torchlight through
the streets of St. Paul. Within 15 years he died a pauper. Decades later a
fellow territorial politician commemorated the events of 1857 by presenting two portraits of him in métis garb, one to the prestigious Minnesota
Club, the other to the Minnesota Historical Society. For generations
since, his exploits have been described in loving detail in books and magazines intended for adults and impressionable young people.[1]

The tale of Joseph Rolette Jr. is one of the key stories that
Minnesotans of generations past have remembered about the territorial
years. It was Rolette, also known as Jolly Joe, who "stole" the bill that
would have moved the capital of Minnesota from St. Paul to St. Peter. It
was also Joe Rolette—sometimes described as a "half breed" —who
brought his dogs into the halls of the capitol, and about whom, when "a
commotion was heard down the street," early residents of St. Paul said:
"Well, it is either a big fire or else Joe Rolette is in town."[2]

What explains the popularity of Rolette—the character—and the
endurance of the legend about the capital bill, an unusual one for a state
that prides itself on clean politics? Perhaps it is simply a colorful, romantic legend, helpful in enlivening otherwise dry accounts of bills written,
debated, and passed. Or perhaps the story provides a much-needed
example of an individual making a difference in a world where commit-
tees and quorums govern. It could be that the legend of Joe Rolette is

Dakota tipis surround the lone frame home of
John H. Stevens near the Falls of St. Anthony, the future site of
Minneapolis's Bridge Square, in this 1854 daguerreotype

like the trickster stories found in the literature of many cultures, designed to amuse and to provide children with examples of otherwise unacceptable behavior.[3]

Whether or not these factors help explain the legend's endurance, the often-described incidents of Rolette's life—many of which seem to have occurred— are succinct records of important themes in the early history of Minnesota. The capital bill itself was the product of the conflict between political factions and economic interests in the territory, played out, in part, in terms of race. The events depend in part on Rolette's perceived status as a half breed, a category that many in the territory considered emblematic of the social, cultural, and political system they sought to remove or replace. Altogether, the legend of Joe Rolette is about culture, politics, race, and power. For these reasons it is worth remembering and reconsidering.

STUDYING THE PRETERRITORIAL PERIOD of Minnesota's history is a little like doing archaeology. Each generation creates a structure of belief and experience that covers up or reinterprets past experiences and past views of the world. This is especially true for generations that undergo great communal experiences such as mass movements, wars, and depressions. Such groups often reinvent the past as a tool for achieving social, political, and cultural change. In doing so, they make it difficult for later generations to understand the lives and experiences of people before the period of massive change. To imagine what life was like in the Minnesota region before 1849 and appreciate the nature of the drastic changes that took place in the 1850s, it is necessary to dig through the deposits of interpretation left by territorial Minnesotans.

In 1853 John Wesley Bond began his classic guidebook, *Minnesota and Its Resources,* with a description designed to reinterpret the region's culture and history: "A very few years ago and the present territory of Minnesota was a waste of woodland and of prairie, uninhabited save by the different hordes of savage tribes from time immemorial scattered through its expanse, with of later years a few white traders only intermingled. At intervals a zealous missionary of the cross, or adventurous traveller, by turns found their way to the Great Falls of St. Anthony."[4]

Found here are some of the basic themes of postterritorial Minnesota history: the region was inhabited by savage, uncivilized, wandering peoples who made wasteful use of the land and were occasionally visited by a few traders, missionaries, and daring adventurers. An early Minnesota politician, William P. Murray, provided an example of the way that these themes came to be copied and embellished. In a 1904 speech to the executive council of the Minnesota Historical Society, he described the territory in 1849 as "little more than a wilderness, a vast waste of prairie and pine lands," a region that was "more remote from settlement and civilization than the most distant part of our country today."[5]

A key concept in Murray's speech was "settlement," the term usually used to describe the process through which European Americans came to inhabit vast regions of the United States. Though the word can simply mean a place where people live and the process by which people move from one region to another, nineteenth-century European Americans used it to describe a culturally specific set of beliefs about proper land use and, more generally, what constituted civilization.[6]

Thus, settlement was not merely the presence of people but the introduction of various features that symbolized Euro-American society and provided the basis for an ordered way of life. Essential to the concept was agriculture, defined as planting crops on a large scale or raising domestic animals. The so-called settlers of the 1850s were, in their terms, engaged in imposing agriculture and the agricultural way of life on an orderless region that they believed to be wasted on its inhabitants.

These beliefs would later provide the basis for the frontier thesis of historian Frederick Jackson Turner. For Turner, settlement was a process of social evolution, of "progress from primitive industrial society without division of labor, up to manufacturing civilization." The frontier was "the meeting point between savagery and civilization," the place where an oncoming movement of people of mainly European origin encountered what was seen as a wilderness, an area of "free land"—that is, land occupied only by Indian people.[7]

While the characteristics used to describe settlement were essentially cultural, race was becoming increasingly important in defining American civilization. More and more Americans in the midnineteenth century believed that human beings could be categorized according to racial groups, not all of which had the same intelligence and capabilities. Those considered superior were described as Anglo-Saxon, Germanic, Caucasian—or, simply, white. Indian people and blacks, as well as, on occasion, Irish, Italians, and others were thought to be inferior and without a part to play in the making of American society. In keeping with these new attitudes, settlement and civilization came to be described as the accomplishments of white people, even if other groups might live an orderly, cultured existence. From this point of view, the history of settlement in the Minnesota region, as described by post-territorial historians, was essentially the story of how Minnesota came to be white.[8]

Murray showed this perspective in his speech when he sought to define which early non-Indian residents of the region were white and which were not. He noted that early in 1849 the "entire white population scarcely exceeded one thousand persons." Later that year, when more immigrants had arrived, a census recorded 4,680 whites, but he stated that many of these individuals were not really white. For example, St. Paul "had a population of some two hundred, a majority of whom were Indian traders, French, and half breeds" and, of the 637 people of Pembina recorded in the 1849 territorial census, "only a small fraction . . . were white." Murray wished to make clear that the people of European ancestry living in Minnesota in 1849—who had been in the region all of their lives and by many definitions would be called settlers—were not white, not part of the great movement of white settlers into the region. They were part of Minnesota's past, not its future.[9]

For almost 200 years before 1849 the Minnesota region was the scene of a complex economic endeavor, the fur trade, that supported an interdependent social system in which Indian people and mostly French traders lived peacefully together, trading and intermarrying.[10] This system—which benefited both Indian people and the European trade—persisted through British and American control, mainly due to the social and cultural continuity in communities of people of French, Indian, and mixed ancestry, later augmented by some British and American fur traders.

The evolution of the social system through generations of the trade was equally complex. Far from being a homogeneous group, the children of intermarriage between European traders and Indian people exhibited a range of cultural possibilities, often related to economic class. Some children were fully incorporated into Indian communities. Others—particularly those of prominent traders—were sent east to be educated and continue in a trading role. Culturally, they were European.

Still other people of mixed ancestry created new identities apart from the context of the trading post or the Indian village. Impetus for this creation came from the amalgamations of the XY and North West Companies in 1805 and the North West and Hudson's Bay Companies in 1821. These consolidations put many people out of work, forcing them and their families to survive through hunting, gathering, and trading, following both European and Indian patterns. In places such as Prairie du Chien, St. Paul, Mendota, Pembina, and the Red River settlement of Manitoba, as well as in areas surrounding trading-post villages throughout the region, people of mixed ancestry and culture created autonomous, diverse communities.[11]

In the midnineteenth century a variety of terms described the new identities of these people of mixed ancestry and cultures. The German ethnographer and geographer Johann G. Kohl noted that the people of Ojibwe-French heritage on Lake Superior referred to themselves with a jesting term, *chicot*—a French-Canadian word for half-burnt stumps. Other phrases were *bois brulé* or *bois grillé* (burned wood or grilled wood), "in reference to the shades of colour that bronze the face of a mixed breed." A newer term, originally used for specific groups of French-Indian people living

Settlers, possibly the Orrocks of Big Lake in present-day Sherburne County, dressed up and posed outside of their log cabin, about 1857

Census enumerator
William W. Warren

on the northern plains and supported by the large herds of buffalo, was *métis*, which simply means "mixed" or "mixed race" in French.[12]

In contrast, the names that English-speaking Americans used for these people—"half breed," "half blood," and "mixed blood"—had racial implications. In some instances these classifications merely described the fact or degree of intermarriage. William W. Warren, an educated man of mixed ancestry himself, wrote a fictional tale in the early 1850s of a fur trader among the Blackfeet, a "halfblood" with a Scottish father and Indian mother.[13] Increasingly, however, these terms, particularly "half breed," were used as slurs, designed to suggest an alleged tainted nature.

The specific meaning of these various designations depended largely on context. The census of Minnesota Territory taken in 1850 provides an opportunity to examine the definitions of the terms "half breed" and "white." Like the census of 1849, the 1850 count was designed to measure the population of non-Indian people. It yielded a total of 6,077 residents. If one accepts the U.S. Department of Indian Affairs' estimates of 31,700 Indian people living in and near the territory in the early 1850s, these 6,077 represented only about 16 percent of the area's total population (see Table 1).[14]

In addition to recording names, sexes, and birthplaces, census enumerators could also note what would now be called racial classifications such as white, black, mulatto, half breed, and Indian (although no Indians were recorded). Some enumerators, such as the fur trader Alexis Bailly, who recorded Wabashaw County, and William Warren, who did Mahkahta and Wahnahta, listed no one as a half breed. In fact, the only racial categories they used were "black" and "mulatto," which meant that they classified all others as white. On the other hand, Jonathan McKusick, a 38-year-old lumberman who had arrived only the year before from Maine, listed a number of families as half breeds in his census of Washington and Itasca Counties. Probably few of the

individuals he identified by this term varied in degree of Indian ancestry from many of the individuals Bailly and Warren recorded as white. In the end, the published 1850 census used only two categories: whites—including all those specifically described by enumerators as half breeds—and free colored (see Table 2).[15]

Clearly, at the time of the 1850 census, the federal government was not concerned with identifying people

TABLE 1
Indian Groups in Minnesota Territory, 1849–53*

Group	Year	Population
Ojibwe		
Lake Superior (Grand Portage, Fond du Lac)	1850	500
St. Croix River (Namekagan, Pokegama, Yellow, and Rice Lakes, Snake River)	1850	800
Mississippi (Sandy Lake, Mille Lacs, Rabbit River, Gull Lake, and other locations)	1850	1,100
Pillagers (Leech Lake, Ottertail Lake)	1850	1,050
Northern or Red Lake (Red Lake, Pembina, Cass Lake, Lake Winnibigoshish)	1850	1,200
Bois Forts (Rainy Lake, Vermilion Lake)	1850	800
Dakota		
Mdewakanton	1849	2,200
Wahpekute	1849	800
Wahpetonwan	1849	1,500
Sisseton	1849	3,800
Yankton	1849	3,200
Yanktonai	1849	4,000
Teton	1849	6,000
Ho-Chunk (Winnebago)	1849	2,500
Mandan, Hidatsa, and Arikara	1853	2,250
Total		**31,700**

* St. Croix Ojibwe, Teton Dakota, Ho-Chunk, and the Mandan, Hidatsa, and Arikara were not contained entirely within Minnesota Territory.

Sources: Statistics compiled by Ken Mitchell and the author from estimates in U.S. Commissioner of Indian Affairs, *Annual Report*, 1849, p. 79, 82, 84–87, 88; 1850, p. 53–59; 1853, p. 116. Groups are categorized as shown in the original sources. For the Wahpekute a range of 600–800 was given.

TABLE 2
Non-Indian Population of Minnesota Territory, 1850

Birthplace	White Male	White Female	Free Colored Male	Free Colored Female	Total
Total U.S. excluding Minnesota	1,612	874	14	11	2,511
Minnesota Territory	776	796	7	7	1,586
Total Foreign Born	1,305	672	0	0	1,977
Unknown	2	1			3
Total	**3,695**	**2,343**	**21**	**18**	**6,077**

Source: United States Census, 1850, p. 993, 996

of European-Indian ancestry. How many were living in the territory? Without a detailed look at the genealogies of those recorded, an actual measure is not possible. Nonetheless, a majority of those listed as being born in Minnesota and the British Red River region may have been of Dakota, Ojibwe, or other Indian ancestry. The sum of these categories suggests that people of Indian-European ancestry may have numbered as many as 2,237, or 37 percent of the territory's population. This figure includes the children of new arrivals and missionaries who had been in the region for some time, but it leaves out residents of mixed ancestry who had been born in Wisconsin, Michigan, Missouri, and other locations (see Table 3). In fact, statistician Joseph A. Wheelock wrote that in 1860 there were 3,475 people of mixed-Indian ancestry in the state. Since the area of the new state was smaller than that of the earlier territory, his larger figure may be the most accurate for 1850. In that case, more than 57 percent of the non-Indian population of Minnesota Territory would have been of mixed-Indian ancestry.[16]

The ways that different enumerators categorized the population of Minnesota Territory shows the contextual nature of the terms "white" and "half breed" and the way in which they evolved. Beginning in 1849, population figures were used to argue for recognition as a territory and, later, as a state. Categorizing people of mixed ancestry as white helped make the case for the territory.

Later on, however, in describing how far Minnesota had come, people like Murray minimized the white population before 1849 in order to emphasize the vast strides made by later settlers. At the same time, it was useful to stress the wild, unusual, foreign quality of the place before large numbers of whites arrived. Territorial Governor Ramsey in an 1853 speech provided an early example of this retrospective view, describing what he

had seen when he first came to St. Paul four years before: "the motley humanity partially filling these streets—the blankets and painted faces of Indians, and the red sashes and moccasins of French voyageurs and half-breeds, greatly predominating over the less picturesque costume of the Anglo-American race."[17]

TABLE 3
Birthplaces of Non-Indian Minnesotans, 1850

Birthplaces	Males	Females	Total
New England States	434	215	649
Middle Atlantic States	511	221	732
Middle Western States	507	366	873
Southern States	151	67	218
Other U.S.	56	34	90
Minnesota Territory	741	768	1509
British Red River	365	363	728
Eastern Canada	490	176	666
Other Foreign Born	461	140	601
Unknown	5	5	10
Total	**3,721**	**2,355**	**6,076**

Source: Statistics compiled by David Hacker from the original 1850 census for the Minnesota Historical Society exhibits program, forthcoming in Steven Ruggles and Matthew Sobek, Integrated Public Use Microdata Series (Minneapolis: Historical Census Projects, University of Minnesota, 1998). This re-compilation produced a total population for the territory of one less than the published figure. This author categorized raw data in the database into the regional groupings shown above. New England states include Connecticut, New Hampshire, Maine, Massachusetts, Rhode Island, and Vermont. Middle Atlantic states: Delaware, New Jersey, New York, and Pennsylvania. Southern states: Alabama, Arkansas, District of Columbia, Georgia, Kentucky, Louisiana, Maryland, North Carolina, South Carolina, Tennessee, and Virginia. Midwestern states: Illinois, Indiana, Iowa, Michigan, Ohio, and Wisconsin.

The early histories of Minnesota's settlement described the many "firsts" accomplished by white people —the first town, church, school, and child born—allegedly producing an orderly region of uniform whiteness in which no racial mixing took place. In these accounts, the presence or accomplishments of people of mixed background were seldom considered relevant.[18]

In reference to such accounts of firsts, George Bonga, a fur trader at Leech Lake and the grandson of a black slave at Mackinac Island who had married an Ojibwe woman, explained how he fit into the world of people who were either white or not white. Bonga "would frequently paralyze his hearers," according to territorial legislator Charles E. Flandrau, "when reminiscing by saying, 'Gentlemen, I assure you that John Banfil [an early St. Paul businessman] and myself were the first two white men that ever came into this country.'" Bonga's witty remark suggests that the term "white" was a relative one, often contrasted with either

"black" or "red." In the Minnesota context, where the contrast between white and red was of prime importance, Bonga, a fur trader and, therefore, culturally non-Indian, had to be white.[19]

Other preterritorial residents of the region made other choices. Ethnographer Kohl noted that even "pure-blooded French Voyageurs" who had lived their entire lives among the Indians and intermarried with them sometimes identified themselves as *chicot* or *bois brulé*. Further, he noted, they "identified themselves with the Indians against the Anglo-Saxons," giving the example of one man who spoke nostalgically about what life was like before *les blancs,* the whites—meaning British, Scottish, Irish, and Yankees—had appeared among them. He missed most, he told Kohl, the songs that people in these communities had known and sung. It was sad, he said, that few people knew them any more.[20]

For this French Canadian, being nonwhite represented a specific society of European and Indian background, one that depended on an interactive social and economic relationship, one that was becoming less and less possible with the changes taking place in the region. Perhaps most significantly, the fur trade itself, which had given birth to this society, was ceasing to exist in its traditional form.

BY THE TIME MINNESOTA became a territory, native Americans were under pressure from the movement to colonize the Great Lakes country. With colonization, Indian people, who had held real power in the fur-trade era, were marginalized, no longer crucial to the survival or profit of Europeans who entered the area.

This process of marginalizing was gradual, and it began with the signing of treaties turning over title to vast areas of land to the U.S. government. Essential to the process was the participation of fur traders and other opportunistic entrepreneurs who created a new form of economic enterprise. In what historian Robert A. Trennert called the "Indian business," Indian people were still the source of profit but received little long-term benefit in return.[21]

The link between the Indian-based fur trade and the Indian business was the traditional credit system wherein Indian people were advanced a variety of trade goods in the fall to be repaid in furs throughout the fall and winter. Short-term variations in climate and in animal populations meant that it was sometimes difficult to repay debts fully. On the other hand, traders had allowed for a certain amount of unpaid credit in the rates of exchange they negotiated. Traders often forgave Indian debts because they were seldom real debts. Nonetheless, in treaties for land signed with Indian people beginning in

Fur trader George Bonga

the 1830s, large trading companies were able to persuade the federal government to allow for repayment of a variety of these often-illusory debts.[22]

For traders—including some of mixed ancestry—these payments were a windfall, an indemnity for losing their business, and the basis of a new kind of endeavor. For the government these payments were essentially a bribe or kickback, a price that had to be paid for the cooperation of traders in negotiating the treaties. Some of the payments may have been justified, but the system spawned new kinds of traders who advanced goods to Indian people in anticipation of treaty signings for the sole purpose of later filing claims for inflated debts.[23]

Claims for debts were not the only ways in which traders profited from the government's system of paying Indian people for their land. Yearly disbursements of goods and money—called annuity payments—provided entrepreneurs with the opportunity to sell items to Indians. Being at the annuity payments also allowed traders to coerce Indian people into repaying debts. In addition, some traders and former trade employees were paid to be interpreters, farmers, or blacksmiths. Others were involved in government contracts to help resettle Indian people on new lands, as required by some of the treaties.

In Minnesota Territory, the Indian business was an industry that not only profited individual companies and entrepreneurs but also fueled the fledgling economy. It was for this reason that the new territorial assembly passed, during its first session in 1849, a resolution asking the government in Washington to remove all Ojibwe living in areas that had been ceded under the treaties of 1837 and 1842. The ostensible reason for this request was to "ensure the security and tranquillity of the white settlements in an extensive and valuable district of this Territory," but the vast majority of these Ojibwe were actually living across the border in the new state of Wisconsin. Their removal would put them entirely within Minnesota Territory, up the Mississippi River from the commercial center of St. Paul.[24]

Comments by prominent participants in the Indian business make clear the hopes attached to this resolution. Former fur trader Henry M. Rice, who had made money in the late 1840s arranging for the removal of the Ho-Chunk (Winnebago) to a reservation they disliked in central Minnesota, told Governor Ramsey in December 1849 that the Ojibwe who lived in Wisconsin and received their annuities at at La Pointe

should be removed from the ceded lands. They should receive their annuities on the Mississippi River, say at or near Sandy Lake, at which place an Agency for the

whole tribe should be established. This would better accommodate the whole tribe and Minnesota would reap the benefit whereas now their annuities pass via Detroit and not one dollar do our inhabitants get altho' we are subject to all the annoyance given by those Indians.[25]

President Zachary Taylor ordered the removal of the Wisconsin Ojibwe into the Upper Mississippi region on February 6, 1850. A participant in the affair, Charles H. Oakes, a former American Fur Company trader on Lake Superior who was then setting up operations in St. Paul, wrote to business ally Henry H. Sibley: "I have received the appointment of removal agent for the Chippeways and hope to be able to make it profitable to the company as the employing of men, furnishing provisions and canoes &c. will necessarily be done through me."[26]

Subsequently, the whole removal effort fell apart from mismanagement and corruption on the part of government officials, not to mention the fact that many Ojibwe died from starvation and disease because of late annuity payments. Finally, the Wisconsin Ojibwe simply refused to remain in Minnesota Territory. Even then, charges made back and forth referred to the loss of potential profit. William Warren, who lived in Benton County, Minnesota Territory, and had been hired to help in the removal, stated that had it been successful, the "money would naturally have found its way down

Trade goods transformed:
Floral embroidery and blue silk ribbon on a
woolen shirt, probably made from a trader's blanket

the Mississippi (the natural channel) and instead of hard times we should have had easy times, and money would have been plenty."[27]

In economic terms, what Warren referred to was the multiplier effect, the widespread result of a government expenditure on the economy. Businessmen who contracted with the government or who dealt directly with Indian people used their money to invest in real estate, to build buildings and houses, to buy, sell, and hire. Each person they paid spread the money around to others, helping to create a Minnesota economy, though little long-term benefit accrued to Indian people themselves.

Understanding of this multiplier effect is evident in a local saying from the early 1850s. As the *Minnesota Pioneer* reported on August 8, 1850: "One would suppose by the promises about town, that the Indian payment would square every debt in Minnesota, but the 'debt of Nature.' Every reply to a dun is, 'after the payment.'"

Alexander Ramsey, in an address to the 1851 legislature, put the matter succinctly: "The payments of the Indian annuities supply much the larger portion of our current currency, and through the various channels of trade contribute greatly to our prosperity." Five years later the *St. Paul Advertiser* provided more detail:

A few years ago the Indian Payments were the great event of the year in Minnesota. Everything in financial matters dated from and was referred to the Indian Payments; almost our whole specie currency was derived from this source. Notes fell due and Grocer's bills matured at the Indian Payment. The persistent dun, the wife's new dress, the ball, the workman, and the new hat, were put off till "after payment."

The article stated that annuity payments—regardless of the welfare of the Indian people who were supposed to benefit from them—were "one of the grand resources of Minnesota," discussed along with "vague hints of exhaustless coal fields and rich lead mines on the Minnesota, and perennial supplies of imaginary pumpkins, two feet in diameter."[28]

Statistics for the 1850s show the importance of Indian expenditures. In his 1860 compilation, J. A. Wheelock stated that from 1849 to 1859 the federal government expended $4.2 million to "fulfill Treaty obligations with Indian tribes." This amounted to more than $380,000 per year, although particular treaties affected the amount each year in different ways. By comparison, expenditures supporting the territorial government, building military roads, and erecting lighthouses and military posts amounted to only $1.2 million, or an average of $120,000 per year, for the same period. No private enterprise in the Minnesota region at the begin-

ning of the 1850s could match the value obtained yearly from Indian expenditures. In 1849 one of the largest of the new businesses, lumbering in the St. Croix River valley, produced logs worth an estimated $150,000. It was not until 1855 that the annual production exceeded $380,000 per year.[29]

By 1856, when other industries had come to rival Indian-related government expenditures, the *St. Paul Advertiser* noted that the expenditures had been important in a population of no more than 30,000 "nibbling for the most part on the edges of the Indian trade." But now that the region's population was 150,000 people involved in "agriculture, manufactures and commerce," no one cared when or where the Indians were paid. According to the newspaper, a single week's business in St. Paul exceeded the yearly payment in cash of $90,000 to the Dakota.[30]

It is clear from this evidence that Indian people, through the money due them for their land, were key in providing an early boost for the Minnesota economy. Without them, economic development would have been greatly slowed. Besides this boost, Indian expenditures shaped Minnesota politics in the territory's initial years. Its key figures—people like Sibley and Rice—owed their economic standing to the profits they made in the Indian business and their political power to their ability to deliver the Indian expenditures to the larger community. Most of the men involved in the Indian business and the political power connected to it were Democrats, as were most Indian traders, a result of the party's long-term control of Indian policy in Washington.[31]

In the early 1850s in Minnesota the major political contests were between Democratic factions eager to have the largest share of the pie. An example was the recurrent competition between Sibley and Rice who, essentially, sought the same political results but differed as to who would receive the economic benefits. The *Minnesota Chronicle and Register* once commented that a controversy over Rice's contract for the removal of the Ho-Chunk in 1850 did not warrant making political capital, since it was simply a "personal quarrel between two rival parties of Indian traders. . . . One party *wanted* the contract—the other *got* it."[32]

Even non-Democrats such as Ramsey, the Whig-appointed territorial governor and superintendent of Indian affairs, participated tacitly, if not always eagerly, in this profitable relationship between politics and the Indian business. In January 1853 the *St. Paul Democrat* condemned the "conclave" of Ramsey and Sibley in the "Sioux Frauds," the wholesale distribution of Indian money from the Dakota treaties of 1851 to a variety of traders.[33] Only with the appointment of Ramsey's re-

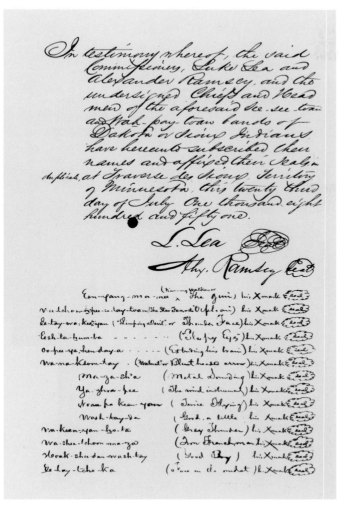

Page of the 1851 Treaty of Traverse des Sioux with signatures of Indian commissioners Luke Lea and Alexander Ramsey and the marks of "chiefs and head men" of the Sisseton and Wahpeton Dakota

placement did successful opposition develop not only to the letting of particular contracts and the distribution of treaty money in certain ways but to the more general, widespread practice of mixing business and Indian policy.

THE 1853 ELECTION of a new Democratic president, Franklin Pierce, brought reform to many policies of previous administrations. Instrumental in carrying out these changes in Minnesota Territory was the new governor, Willis A. Gorman, a lawyer, former and future military officer, and congressman, who was appointed in March. From the beginning, Gorman made it clear that he was unhappy with the way in which Indian policy had been carried out in Minnesota. He sought to cut off the access by businessmen of his own party to federal Indian money.

In the summer of 1853 Gorman took part in a congressional investigation of Ramsey's actions in negotiating the Dakota treaties of 1851. On August 8, 1853, Gorman negotiated a new treaty with the Ho-Chunk that shifted their reservation to a location more to their liking and left out payments to traders for past debts. That fall he took steps to terminate remnants of the policy of forcing Wisconsin Ojibwe to move to Minnesota.[34]

Needless to say, by the end of 1853 Gorman had earned many enemies in his own party, particularly Rice, who had been elected in October to replace Sibley as territorial delegate in Congress.[35] Rice was able to block ratification of the Ho-Chunk treaty, and rumors were circulating in Washington that Gorman's power over Indian matters would be curtailed by a separation of the duties of territorial governor and superintendent of Indian affairs, something that had been accomplished in other territories.

Gorman wrote to an official in Washington explaining the difficulties he had encountered in Minnesota due to his opposition to the people who had "fattened for 25 years upon the Indians and the U. S. Treasury." He stated: "These men are evidently in hopes of getting some one here who can be used by them. Now I need not tell you that there is or has been more fraud and cheating in the Indian trade in the Territory than it has been my lot to see or know of any where else on earth." This "interest," he explained, was represented by Rice. When he first arrived in the territory, Gorman had supported Rice's election as territorial delegate because they were fellow Democrats. But Rice had claims against the Ho-Chunk that he sought to have included in the treaty, and Gorman had not backed him. Gorman stated: "I don't suit him. I have declined his overtures in Indian matters."[36]

Changes in the territory's population provided more backing for Gorman's positions. Between 1855 and 1857 the population grew from 40,000 to 150,000. These new settlers came primarily from the Middle Atlantic states, New England, and the

Former Territorial Governor Willis A. Gorman, about 1866

Midwest. While figures from the pre-statehood census of 1857 have not been compiled, the influx from these regions is apparent in the 1860 federal census, taken after an additional 22,000 people had arrived in Minnesota. At that date, individuals from the three regions (excluding Minnesota) totaled 75,499, or 44 percent of the state's population (see Tables 4 and 5). These individuals settled in large numbers in southeastern Minnesota and became the base for the new Republican Party, begun in the state in 1855. Despite being a Democrat, Gorman aligned himself with the Republicans in a major debate of the time concerning the ultimate borders of Minnesota, the state-to-be.[37]

The impressive growth in Minnesota's population created an impetus for statehood. In pushing for it, congressional delegate Rice favored a new western boundary roughly like the current one. In the territory, however, there was a strong sentiment, especially among southern Minnesotans, in favor of dividing it along an east-west line around the 45th (just north of the Twin Cities) or 46th parallels (just north of Little Falls).[38]

Economic interests shaped the opposing positions. For businessmen based in St. Paul with backgrounds in the Indian trade, like Rice and his supporters, the north-south state would include a vast northern region where the trade that had brought them money and power could continue. To keep profiting from the intersection of business and Indian money, Rice himself needed to have political power in the same governmental entity in which he carried on trade.

The many newcomers and Republicans in southern Minnesota, who believed the future lay in agriculture, saw that a horizontally shaped state would isolate St. Paul near the northern border and strengthen the

TABLE 4
Birthplaces of Minnesotans in 1860 Census

Birthplace	Population
U.S. Outside of Minnesota	
New England	18,822
Middle Atlantic States	30,075
Middle West	26,602
Other U.S.	3,491
Subtotal	*78,990*
Minnesota	34,305
Total Born in U.S.	**113,295**
Foreign Born	
Canada	8,023
British Isles	17,798
Europe	32,788
Other Foreign Born	119
Total Foreign Born	**58,728**
Total Population	**172,023**

Sources: United States Census, 1860, Population, 253, 254, 261, 262. Figures are for all so-called races and colors.

hand of agricultural interests. Governor Gorman aligned himself with the Republicans on this issue, a logical extension of his opposition to the corruption endemic in the Indian business.

These new political interests did not seek to eliminate any role for federal government in fostering private enterprise. Rather, they sought their subsidies in different ways such as railroad grants, another important issue at the time. The capital-removal bill that Rolette confiscated was still another example. Not content to wait for action in Washington, Gorman and the Republicans sought to further their position by moving the capital of the territory to a town more centrally located in the state they hoped to create: St. Peter, on the Minnesota River. Gorman himself invested in the company hoping to develop the new capital—a form of graft and a conflict of interest or simply an indication of the depth of his feeling, depending on how one looked at it. Gorman was quoted in the *Daily Minnesotian* as saying that he hoped to see "grass grow in the business streets of St.

TABLE 5
Racial Categories of Minnesotans in 1860 Census

	Native Born		Foreign Born		
	Males	**Females**	**Males**	**Females**	**Totals**
White	60,176	52,872	32,782	25,934	171,764
Black	39	51			90
Mulatto	80	77	7	5	169
Totals	**60,295**	**53,000**	**32,789**	**25,939**	**172,023**

Sources: U.S. Census, 1860, Population, 253, 254, 261, 262.

Figures for the white population include 2,369 Indians, who were elsewhere located by county of residence, though not identified by place of birth. Of this total, 1,274 were living in Pembina (later Kittson) County. They were not Indians on reservations but, rather, people of Indian ancestry—whether considered full or mixed blood—living in white communities.

Paul in two years."[39] The bill passed both houses of the assembly and seemed poised for signing. It was then, according to the legend of Joe Rolette, that the "jolly half breed" performed his heroic acts.

THE MANY AND VARIED VERSIONS of Rolette's adventures bear the mark of continuous telling and retelling during the late-nineteenth century. There are so many versions of the story that it is difficult to know what actually happened in 1857 and what was embroidered by later storytellers. It is also not always clear whose purposes were served by the various versions and emphases on particular aspects of the legend. It is worthwhile examining some of the patterns to see what was included as well as what was left out.

A major feature of some accounts is the suggestion that Rolette was a rough frontiersman. This is hard to match with the actual experiences of his life. His father was a successful and well-educated trader from French Canada, responsible for the American Fur Company's entire upper Mississippi region in the 1820s. As a boy, Joseph had been educated at a private school in New York City, under the protection of American Fur Company president Ramsay Crooks. Whatever the details of his experience in New York, it is hard to believe the accuracy of the legend that describes Rolette arriving there dressed in a full suit of buckskin and carrying a rifle over his shoulder.[40]

An equally misleading part of the Rolette legend is the suggestion that he was a half breed or mixed blood. Political journalist and historian Harlan P. Hall noted that, though he was "commonly supposed to be a half or quarter breed Frenchman," he was instead a "full-blooded French Canadian." More recently, historian Rhoda R. Gilman wrote that Rolette's heritage was almost entirely French and British, his "only traceable Indian ancestor being an Ottawa great-great-great-grandmother."[41]

Rolette's association with the Pembina community began in the 1840s, following the completion of his education, when he went to work for Sibley in the crucial northern border region along the Red River where the American Fur Company competed with the British Hudson's Bay Company. Rolette appears to have done his job well and was instrumental in initiating the commerce involving Red River oxcart trains bringing furs and buffalo skins from the northern plains to St. Paul. It was this commerce that essentially made St. Paul the key commercial center of the region.[42]

Rolette's tie to the Pembina community came about in part through his marriage to a métis woman, Angélique Jerome, following a pattern traditional for

Joseph Rolette Jr., portrayed as a métis in this pastel by an unknown artist, about 1890

THE MOST FAMOUS IMAGE of Joseph Rolette Jr. is a pastel showing him in métis garb, wearing leggings, a blanket coat, and a decorated bandolier bag or shoulder pouch. There are two copies of this portrait, presented by fellow territorial politician Charles E. Flandrau to the Minnesota Historical Society and St. Paul's Minnesota Club in April 1890. Flandrau later wrote: "As I admired the plucky manner in which my friend had stood by St. Paul in this the hour of her danger, I conceived the idea of preserving the event to history by presenting his portrait to the Historical Society . . . and hung one in the Minnesota Club. It is a capital likeness, representing him, full-life size, in the wild and picturesque costume of the border. A brass tablet on the frame is inscribed with the following legend: 'The Hon. Joe Rolette, who saved the capital to St. Paul, by running away with the bill removing it to St. Peter, in 1857.'"

Flandreau may have commissioned the pastels around 1890 as part of his attempts to memorialize Rolette, who died in 1871. The image may have been copied from an earlier photograph; one showing Rolette, seated and wearing a blanket coat and bandolier bag (though of different design), is in the historical society's collections (detail above). A woodcut from this image was used to illustrate several accounts of the Rolette legend (*Northwest Magazine*, Feb. 1888; *St. Paul Dispatch*, Feb. 10, 1894). The photograph bears a handwritten caption, probably from the nineteenth century, identical to the words on the portrait's brass plaque.

traders interested in carrying on business with native communities.[43] Associated in business with Sibley, Rolette was in a good position to be a broker, delivering benefits from Sibley to the métis and political support from the large métis community to Sibley.

The 1850 census gives some indication of the size of the métis population, showing 1,134 people living in Pembina County—almost 19 percent of the territory's entire population. Not all county residents were métis; while some were listed as being born at Pembina, many others were natives of the British Red River colony or eastern Canada. One way or another, by the standards of Johann Kohl's Lake Superior informants, they appear to have identified culturally and politically with the interests that Joseph Rolette represented.[44]

From the beginning of the territory, the métis sought to influence the new government. A petition from the "Half-Breeds of Pembina," sent sometime in 1849 and signed by a number of people including Rolette, asked Governor Ramsey to use his influence to establish courts and civil officials in the region, to exclude British subjects from hunting there, to erect a fort to protect the border, and to arrange for the sale of land from Indians to the métis so that residents could obtain clear title to their land.[45]

Despite their interest in government, not all of the people of the Pembina region were able to participate in the initial elections of territorial legislators. The congressional act providing for the organization of the territory stated that voters in the first election were limited to "free white male inhabitants" over the age of 21 who had lived in the territory when the act was passed and were citizens of the United States. The territorial legislature was empowered to determine voter qualifications in later elections. In the fall of 1849 a bill passed that provided that "all persons [men] of a mixture of white and Indian blood and who shall have adopted the habits and customs of civilized men, are hereby declared to be entitled to all the rights and privileges" of voting.[46]

If not immediately represented among the white voters of the territory, the métis were also not categorized as Indian people able to participate in treatymaking. As a result of the prompting in the métis petition, the federal government, in 1851, authorized Ramsey to negotiate the purchase of land in the Pembina region. When he arrived there he discovered that the métis wished to be signatories of the treaty, alleging, according to Ramsey, "that it was they who possessed the Country really, and who had long defended and maintained it against the encroachments of enemies." Ramsey wrote that "on the policy of the government and the impracticability of its treating with its own

Métis drivers and their oxcarts, pictured as one of the "gems of Minnesota scenery" by Whitney's Gallery, St. Paul, 1860

quasi citizens being explained to them, they were satisfied that their demands could not be complied with." Nonetheless, Ramsey saw that the treaty included a provision allowing this "interesting and peculiar people" in a "peculiar situation" to receive $30,000. Unfortunately for the métis, the Pembina treaty failed to pass Congress in 1852.[47]

Ramsey's dealings with these "peculiar" "qausi citizens" is in keeping with the general inability of other European Americans to know what to make of the métis but to make use of them when needed. This may explain why the law was passed in 1849 allowing people of mixed ancestry to vote. The Pembina district, represented by Joseph Rolette and his fellow trader Norman

Kittson beginning in 1852, provided support to Sibley's "conclave" in the territorial legislature. In 1853, for example, Rolette took pleasure in reporting to Sibley's brother Frederick that he had prevented Rice from receiving many votes in Pembina.[48]

Rolette's legislative career between 1852 and 1857 has never been explored in much detail. One memorable anecdote is Murray's account of Kittson's and Rolette's first trip to the legislature in January 1852, an 18-day journey by dogsled. "For the first few days of the session it was hard to tell whether it was the dogs or the honorable members who represented Pembina, as the dogs were the first in the legislative halls and the last to leave, and it was only when the sergeant at arms was ordered to put the dogs out and keep them out, as Pembina was not entitled to double representation, that the two houses were relieved of their presence."[49]

In contrast to this light-hearted story, some of Rolette's actions as a territorial legislator suggest that he tried to further the interests of people of Indian ancestry in the region. On January 18, 1856, for example, Rolette introduced a memorial to Congress calling for changes in federal laws in order to extend citizenship to Indian people who had altered their "habits and mode of life." Written in the rhetoric of the time, which equated patterns of subsistence and types of clothing with civilization, the resolution stated, "By granting the right of citizenship . . . a great step would be gained in the progress of the tribes around us, in the path of civilization." The memorial noted that although an Indian person "assumed the dress of the white man, and by his industry has opened himself a farm," as he might have been urged by missionaries and other whites, he could not under current law own the land on which he farmed or "enjoy any of the many franchizes [sic] and privileges which his mode of life and knowledge of our institutions should secure to him." It is not known how much of the resolution Rolette actually wrote, but the memorial, which passed both bodies of the territorial legislature, clearly reflected the belief common among people of mixed ancestry that cultural attributes were more important than so-called racial background.[50]

In addition, Rolette did not initially agree with Rice's 1856 proposal for the north-south shape of the state-to-be. His reaction was based on his relationship with the community he represented. At the beginning of 1856 he introduced a resolution calling for a division of the territory on an east-west line, apparently on the theory, as chronicler Arthur J. Larsen wrote, that this "would place his district in a commanding position in the northern half." The measure was defeated.[51]

Exactly how or in what way Rolette came to change his position on the borders is not clear. His motivation for carrying off the capital bill is left vague in most accounts. This ambiguity is a necessary part of the legend.

CONTRARY TO MANY VERSIONS of the story, Rolette did not actually steal the bill, since, as chairman of the Territorial Council's Committee on Enrolled Bills, he had rightful possession of it after it passed. His duty was simply to certify the text so that it could be sent to the governor for signing. When the bill came into his hands on or before Saturday, February 28, 1857, Rolette simply stayed away from the proceedings. While he was gone, a call of the Council was issued, requiring the presence of all members. Since Rolette could not be found, the Council was prevented from taking further action unless a two-thirds vote dispensed with the call. Since this vote fell one short, the Council was required to remain in session during the call, day and night, until 1:00 P.M. Thursday, March 5—a total of 123 hours. The journal of the final session on March 7 contains a report stating that the Committee on Enrolled Bills had been unable to report back the bill "owing to the absence of the Chairman," that is, Rolette, who was one of the report's signers. Further, the committee related that "numerous errors" were found in comparing copies of the bill. The committee therefore retained the bill in its possession "subject to the order of the Council."[52]

Some variations in the versions of the legend concern minor details, such as which hotel and in which room Rolette stayed during the 123 hours. More significant were the disagreements about the degree of planning and purpose he exhibited and whether or not other powerful people in St. Paul were involved in his actions. Usually this part of the story is murky.

Clearly, what Rolette did was in the interests of St. Paul. During the time he was missing, a duplicate copy of the bill was passed and signed by the governor. Later on in the year, a St. Paul judge ruled that the bill had not properly passed. It is probable that, had it passed in the normal manner, grounds would have been found to overrule it for other reasons.[53]

Nonetheless, most versions of the legend insist that Rolette acted spontaneously. Hall declared, "It is due both Rolette and the citizens of St. Paul to say that no previous or corrupt arrangement was made with him to perform the role which was enacted." Charles Flandrau —despite his description of Rolette's "free and easy, half-savage characteristics"—made clear that he acted in his own interests as well as those of the business community of which he was a part: "It was at this point in the fight that Rolette proved himself a bold and successful strategist. He was a friend of St. Paul, and was determined that the plan should not succeed if it was possible for him to prevent it." J. Fletcher Williams suggested that for Rolette, who had seen the opposition to the bill in St. Paul, "a wink was as good to him as a nod." Historian William Watts Folwell, on the other hand, implied that Rolette was put up to his actions by influential people: "Of a romantic and jovial disposition, he was not at all averse to playing the part assigned him in this little drama." It is unclear whether Folwell was writing in a flowery manner or meant that the events had been scripted by someone else. In any case, although the accounts differ as to the degree of planning or participation, it is clear that many people in St. Paul knew what Rolette was doing while he was doing it.[54]

One way or another, the emphasis in all these stories is that Rolette was an unreflective, humorous, fun-loving, carousing, rough frontiersman—occasionally a half breed or mixed blood. These are the crucial details that help explain the Rolette legend and its hold on post-territorial Minnesota history.

WRITING OF CLASSICAL LEGENDS, Henry David Thoreau stated, "To some extent mythology is only the most ancient history and biography. So far from being false or fabulous in the common sense, it contains only enduring and essential truth, the I and you, the here and there, the now and then, being omitted."[55]

For each generation, legends based on real and invented historical figures serve particular truths and memorialize particular views of the world. More than simply the story of a trickster, the Rolette legend describes a culture hero of the kind found in the literature of many societies: one who performs significant deeds out of hunger, curiosity, or recklessness; a primitive entrepreneur who makes possible the world as it is known and then obligingly disappears.[56]

The truths that Rolette serves come out of the historical context of territorial Minnesota: the replacement of one cultural system by another, rival politicians seeking to capture Indian payments for the local economy, attempts by later reformers to close off this mixture of money and politics (in order to replace it with other forms of business-government collusion), and debates about the shape of the state-to-be. The Rolette legend is, largely, nonpartisan. It serves the purposes of both sides, providing each with a vehicle to record its own views of the world and the nature of territorial Minnesota.

For legislators and St. Paulites who wanted the city to remain the commercial center of the state and who owed their success to the Indian business, the legend's characterization of Rolette is a useful one. Perhaps most significantly, it absolves influential and ordinary people

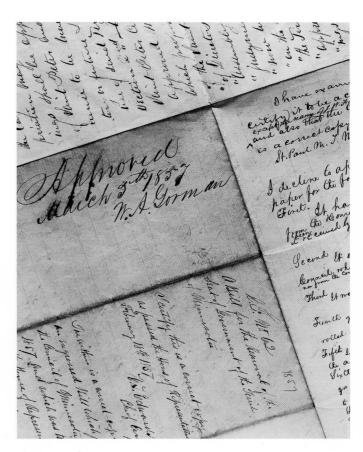

Duplicate bill to remove the capital to St. Peter, certified a "correct copy" and approved by Governor Gorman

from any accountability for a reckless, illegal action that deprived a democratic majority in both legislative houses of the right to pass a bill that the governor was ready to sign. While it would have been better for the drama had Rolette actually been a half breed, it was enough for him to play the part. This identification provided a cultural or racial cover for the actions that Rolette took, in the same way that a group of English colonists in Boston in 1775 dressed as Indians to protest the stamp tax while throwing tea into Boston Harbor.

It was equally useful for those who opposed the role of the Indian traders in Minnesota Territory to categorize Rolette as a reckless half breed. Half breeds symbolized the society that had existed before 1849, as well as the power of the businessmen associated with the Indian trade. One opponent of this power structure later wrote: "Such was the mixed character of the population at the time that a large proportion of the citizens were either by ties of consanguinity, or trading interest, allied to the Indians and their interests; and these were known and designated as the 'Moccasin Democracy or Indian Dynasty.'" Thus, opposition to a certain set of political positions became associated with race and an assertion of white identity. It was easy to blame "half breeds" like Rolette, even though his action benefited mixed bloods less than it did powerful figures in the community, people like Rice and Sibley whose corruption was anything but fun-loving yet who would go on to become revered founding fathers in the story of Minnesota.[57]

Henry H. Sibley, who had just completed his term as governor when painted by T. C. Healy, 1860

Another event of 1857 shows how the so-called half breeds were both used to further the assertion of white identity and blamed for actions that, in fact, benefited the territory's elite. In October 1857 Sibley, running against Ramsey, was elected the first state governor. Commentator Hall noted that the election was extremely close; the many contested ballots in the southern part of the state, as they were counted, put the result in doubt though suggesting strongly that Ramsey would win. When the election results were received from the Cass and Pembina districts, "where Joe Rolette reigned supreme," the tally was "very unanimous for Sibley, giving him in Pembina 316 votes and in Cass 228, while Ramsey did not receive a vote in either county." This helped provide the final majority of 240 for Sibley.[58]

Hall implied that these results were fraudulent, not because they were tampered with, as the unanimous result might suggest. Rather, he explained, the territorial election law, providing that people of mixed white and Indian ancestry "who shall have adopted the habits and customs of civilized men" would be allowed to vote, "practically conferred the right of suffrage upon all the [male] half-breeds in the territory." Hall alleged that this provision was interpreted by election judges to mean that "half-breeds wearing pantaloons filled the requirement. A tradition has come down to later generations to the effect that one pair of pants would do service for a swarm of half-breeds. One would don the trousers and go out and vote, and, soon coming back, passed the garment over to the next man, while he resumed his breech clout and blanket."[59]

Despite his intended slur on people of mixed ancestry, Hall suggested that allowing them to vote was a necessity: "But what else could you do? We had to have a governor, and inhabitants of Scandinavian countries had not then moved into Minnesota.

Consequently, somebody had to do the voting, and in the emergency the half-breed, if he could borrow a pair of pants, was as good as anybody else." Hall's implication was that, by 1904 when he was writing, the emergency was past. Scandinavians were achieving political power. Minnesota had become "white," a region with a reinvented past that did not include Indian people or the Europeans who had lived with them in an era of interdependence. Race had become all-important. In this new Minnesota there was little room for the complex identity of people of mixed ancestry. Instead, the half breed would become a historical character, a transitional figure in the evolution of

the frontier, a creature of legend, a symbol of a time when Minnesota had not attained its later state of whiteness.

Rolette personally shared the fate of the preterritorial Minnesota he symbolized. Having served the purposes of the rich and powerful, he died in 1871 without political power, in obscure but colorful celebrity. From the revisionist point of view of those who have written much of Minnesota's history in the last 150 years, Joe Rolette, like Indians, half breeds, fur traders, voyageurs, and other beings of the mythic prehistory of Minnesota, lives forever, but only in stereotype and legend.[60]

NOTES

[1] The author would like to thank Alan Woolworth for help in researching this topic, Rhoda Gilman for her help and encouragement, and Ken Mitchell, Brian Horrigan, Andrea Cutting, and David Hacker for their help in compiling the statistics.

Major versions of the Rolette legend based on the memories of his contemporaries include Manton Marble, "To the Red River and Beyond," *Harper's New Monthly Magazine* 21 (Oct. 1860): 582; T. M. Newson, *Pen Pictures of St. Paul, Minnesota* (St. Paul: the author, 1886), 683–85; "Joseph Rolette," *Northwest Magazine*, Feb. 1888, p. 22; "Jolly Jo Rolette," *St. Paul Dispatch*, Feb. 10, 1894; H. P. Hall, "Observations," *Minneapolis Journal*, Apr. 13, 1896, and *Observations: Being More or Less a History of Political Contests in Minnesota from 1849 to 1904* (St. Paul: n.p., 1904), 28–36; Charles E. Flandrau, *The History of Minnesota and Tales of the Frontier* (St. Paul: E. W. Porter, 1900), 358–64; William B. Dean, "A History of the Capitol Buildings of Minnesota, with Some Account of the Struggles for Their Location," in *Minnesota Historical Society Collections* 12 (St. Paul, 1908): 9–15; "Bill for Removal of Capital," *St. Paul Dispatch*, May 3, 1911. One version for young people is Roy P. Johnson, "Joe Rolette and the Capital Scandal," in *Gopher Reader*, ed. A. Hermina Poatgieter and James T. Dunn (St. Paul: Minnesota Historical Society [MHS], 1966), 263–65. Newspaperman Merle Potter included the Rolette legend as the first in his well-known *101 Best Stories of Minnesota* (Minneapolis: Harrison and Smith Co., 1931), 1–3.

[2] *St. Paul Dispatch,* Feb. 10, 1894.

[3] On the educational functions of such stories, see Thomas W. Overholt and J. Baird Callicott, *Clothed-in-Fur: An Introduction to an Ojibwa World View* (Washington, D.C.: University Press of America, 1982), 25–26, 145–46; Stith Thompson, *The Folktale* (Berkeley: University of California Press, 1977), 319, 386.

[4] John Wesley Bond, *Minnesota and Its Resources* (New York: Redfield, 1853), 1.

[5] William P. Murray, "Recollections of Early Territorial Days and Legislation," in *Minnesota Historical Society Collections* 12 (St. Paul, 1908): 103. Many travelers' accounts emphasized the dangers posed by Indian people, often greatly exaggerated. See Bruce M. White, "Encounters with Spirits: Ojibwa and Dakota Theories about the French and Their Merchandise," *Ethnohistory* 41 (Summer 1994): 387–89.

[6] Alexander Ramsey, in an 1853 speech to the legislature, made the common assumption that settlers were farmers: "The whole country . . . has the deepest interest in increasing the amount of this cultivation; and the most effectual way of doing this would seem to be by gratuitous grants of land in limited quantities to actual settlers"; Minnesota Territory, *Journal of the House*, 1853, p. 70.

[7] Frederick Jackson Turner, *The Frontier in American History* (New York: Henry Holt and Co., 1920), 3.

[8] On the cultural attributes of the term "white" and its mean-

ing in nineteenth-century America, see David R. Roediger, *The Wages of Whiteness: Race and the Making of the American Working Class* (London: Verso, 1991); Reginald Horsman, *Race and Manifest Destiny: The Origins of American Racial Anglo-Saxonism* (Cambridge, Mass.: Harvard University Press, 1981), 154–55, 189.

[9] Murray, "Recollections," 12: 103–04. Murray's claim of 4,680 whites does not match the commonly accepted total of 4,535; see William W. Folwell, *A History of Minnesota* (St. Paul: MHS, 1956), 1:351–52.

[10] On such intermarriage, see Jennifer S. H. Brown, *Strangers in Blood: Fur Trade Company Families in Indian Country* (Vancouver: University of British Columbia Press, 1980), 51–110; Sylvia Van Kirk, *"Many Tender Ties": Women in Fur-Trade Society, 1670–1870* (Norman: University of Oklahoma Press, 1983), 74–94; Bruce M. White, "The Woman Who Married a Beaver: Trade Patterns and Gender Roles in the Ojibwa Fur Trade," forthcoming in *Ethnohistory*. For the history and origins of the mixed Indian-European society in the Great Lakes, see Jacqueline Peterson, "The People In Between: Indian-White Marriage and the Genesis of a Métis Society and Culture in the Great Lakes Region, 1680–1830" (Ph.D. diss., University of Illinois, 1981).

[11] The term "freemen" was used to describe former fur-trade employees not under contract to large companies who continued to reside in Indian country; see Jacqueline Peterson and Jennifer S. H. Brown, eds., *The New Peoples: Being and Becoming Métis in North America* (Winnipeg: University of Manitoba Press, 1985), 81, 176.

[12] Johann G. Kohl, *Kitchi-Gami: Life Among the Lake Superior Ojibway* (1860; reprint, St. Paul: MHS Press, 1985), 260. For one of the earliest uses of "métis" in this context, see Edmund C. Bray and Martha C. Bray, eds., *Joseph Nicollet on the Plains and Prairies: The Expeditions of 1838–39 With Journals, Letters, and Notes on the Dakota Indians* (St. Paul: MHS Press, 1976), 187–89. See also John Francis McDermott, *A Glossary of Mississippi Valley French, 1673–1850,* Washington University Studies, New Series, No. 12 (St. Louis, 1941), 103. "Métis" is now sometimes used to refer to all people of mixed Indian-European ancestry.

[13] William Warren, "Adventures among the Blackfeet Indians," *Minnesota Chronicle and Register* (St. Paul), Feb. 23, 1850.

[14] For estimates of Indian population, see Table 1. For the non-Indian census, see Patricia C. Harpole and Mary D. Nagle, eds., *Minnesota Territorial Census, 1850* (St. Paul: MHS, 1972), viii–ix. In 1862 statistician Joseph A. Wheelock explained, "The United States census does not regard the Indian tribes as a social constituent of the nation, and therefore takes no account of them in their tribal or savage state"; Minnesota Bureau of Statistics, *Minnesota: Its Progress and Capabilities* (St. Paul: William R. Marshall, 1862), 106–07.

[15] Harpole and Nagle, eds., *Minnesota Territorial Census,* viii, 71–99; *United States Census,* 1850, p. 993, 996.

[16] Minnesota Bureau of Statistics, *Minnesota,* 107.

[17] Minnesota Territory, *Journal of the House,* 1853, p. 74.

[18] See, for example, Edward D. Neill, *History of Washington County and the St. Croix Valley* (Minneapolis: North Star Publishing Co., 1881), 255. Neill also describes a "settlement of half-breeds," all unnamed, at Lakeland.

[19] Charles E. Flandrau, "Reminiscences of Minnesota during the Territorial Period," in *Minnesota Historical Society Collections* 9 (St. Paul, 1901): 199, which states that Bonga was unaware of any categories except white and Indian, suggesting that his statement was naive. It is hard to imagine this to be the case. Bonga was not an ignorant man; like other children of North West Company traders, he was educated in Montreal. As a trader, he sought to imitate the lifestyle of a North West Company bourgeois.

[20] Kohl, *Kitchi-Gami,* 260–61.

[21] Robert A. Trennert Jr., *Indian Traders on the Middle Border: The House of Ewing, 1827–54* (Lincoln: University of Nebraska Press, 1981), 205–10.

[22] Royce Kurtz, "Looking at the Ledgers: Sauk and Mesquakie Trade Debts," in Jennifer S. H. Brown, W. J. Eccles, and Donald P. Heldman, eds., *The Fur Trade Revisited: Selected Papers of the Sixth North American Fur Trade Conference, Mackinac Island, Michigan, 1991* (East Lansing: Michigan State University Press, 1994), 143–59; Trennert, *Indian Traders,* 110. Under the 1837 treaty with the Ojibwe, $70,000 and "other just demands" for claims were included to be paid to traders William A. Aitkin and Lyman M. Warren. A schedule of 55 claims totaling $75,000 was included in the 1842 treaty, some $24,000 of this for John Jacob Astor and another $13,000 for the American Fur Company; Charles J. Kappler, comp., *Indian Affairs. Laws and Treaties* (Washington, D.C.: Government Printing Office, 1904), 2: 482–85, 542–45.

[23] For commentary about the newer traders, see, for example, Samuel W. Pond, *The Dakota or Sioux in Minnesota As They Were in 1834* (1908; reprint, St. Paul: MHS Press, 1986), 173.

[24] Minnesota Territorial Assembly, Resolution, Oct. 11, 1849, in Office of Indian Affairs, Letters Received, Minnesota Superintendency, National Archives microfilm M234, Roll 428, Frames 124–128, copy in MHS; Bruce M. White, "The Regional Context of the Removal Order of 1850," report prepared for the Mille Lacs Band of Ojibwe for *Mille Lacs v. Minnesota,* Dec. 1993, forthcoming in James McClurken, comp., *Fish in the Lakes, Wild Rice, and Game in Abundance: Testimony on Behalf of Mille Lacs Ojibwe Hunting and Fishing Rights.*

[25] At the same time, Rice was campaigning to remove the Menominee as well; Rice to Ramsey, Dec. 1, 1849, in Alexander Ramsey Papers, microfilm edition, Roll 4, Frame 284, MHS.

[26] White, "Removal Order"; Kappler, comp., *Indian Affairs, Laws and Treaties* (1941), 5:663; Charles Oakes to Henry H. Sibley, June 14, 1850, in Henry H. Sibley Papers, microfilm edition, Roll 7, Frame 379, MHS.

[27] *Minnesota Democrat* (St. Paul), Dec. 9, 1851.

[28] *St. Paul Advertiser,* Dec. 6, 1856.

[29] Minnesota Bureau of Statistics, *Minnesota: Its Place Among the States* (Hartford: Case, Lockwood, and Co., 1860), 168. These values are based on William H. C. Folsom's estimate that timber cut in the St. Croix valley was worth $3 per thousand feet of logs; see Folsom, "Lumbering in the St. Croix Valley, with Biographic Sketches," in *Minnesota Historical Society Collections* 9 (St. Paul, 1901): 321–23.

[30] *St. Paul Advertiser*, Dec. 6, 1856.

[31] Charles D. Gilfillan, "The Early Political History of Minnesota," in *Minnesota Historical Society Collections* 9: 177.

[32] *Minnesota Chronicle and Register,* June 10, 1850.

[33] *St. Paul Democrat,* Jan. 12, 1853.

[34] Folwell, *History of Minnesota*, 1:462–70, 478–82.

[35] Folwell, *History of Minnesota*, 1: 373.

[36] Gorman to unnamed, Dec. 17, 1853, in Willis A. Gorman and Family Papers, MHS.

[37] Folwell, *History of Minnesota*, 1: 360, 375; Arthur J. Larsen, "Admission to the Union," *Minnesota History* 14 (June 1933): 159; John G. Rice, "The Old-Stock Americans," in *They Chose Minnesota: A Survey of the State's Ethnic Groups*, ed. June D. Holmquist (St. Paul: MHS Press, 1981), 59, 62.

[38] Here and two paragraphs below, Larsen, "Admission," 157.

[39] *Daily Minnesotian* (St. Paul), Mar. 3, 1857.

[40] Rhoda R. Gilman, Carolyn Gilman, and Deborah M. Stultz, *The Red River Trails: Oxcart Routes Between St. Paul and the Selkirk Settlement, 1820–1870* (St. Paul: MHS, 1979), 18; *St. Paul Dispatch*, Feb. 10, 1894.

[41] Hall, *Observations*, 28; Gilman et al., *Red River Trails*, 18. For a description of Rolette as a mixed blood, see Folwell, *History of Minnesota,* 1: 386.

[42] Gilman et al., *Red River Trails*, 11; *St. Paul Dispatch*, Feb. 10, 1894; J. Fletcher Williams, *A History of the City of Saint Paul to 1875* (1876; reprint, St. Paul: MHS Press, 1983), 160.

[43] Although her obituary, *Kittson County Enterprise*, Feb. 16, 1906, and many other sources list her name as Angelie, the parish register of Assumption Church, Pembina, N.D., (original in possession of church) consistently spells it Angélique. See, for example, the entry for the baptism of her son Henry, Sept. 19, 1857. A note on her photograph, donated to MHS in 1909, states that her first name was Angeline and that she was of Cree and French blood.

[44] *U.S. Census*, 1850, p. 993.

[45] Minnesota Territory, *Journal of the Council*, 1849, p. 197–99.

[46] Minnesota Territory, *Acts, Joint Resolutions, and Memorials*, 1849, p. 6. For the act creating the territory, see Minnesota Territory, *Journal of the House*, 1849, p. 188–93.

[47] Alexander Ramsey to A. H. Stuart, Nov. 7, 1851, in Office of Indian Affairs, Letters Received, Minnesota Superintendency microfilm M234, Roll 428, Frames 371–80; Folwell, *History of Minnesota*, 1: 290–91, 305.

[48] Gilman et al., *Red River Trails*, 18; Joseph Rolette Jr. to F. B. Sibley, Sept. 20, 1853, Sibley papers.

[49] Murray, "Recollections," 118–19.

[50] Minnesota Territory, *Journal of the Council*, 1856, p. 72, and *Session Laws*, 1856, p. 354.

[51] Larsen, "Admission," 158. The title or text of Rolette's resolution has not been found.

[52] Minnesota Territory, *Journal of the Council*, 1857, p. 176–84.

[53] Folwell, *History of Minnesota*, 1: 386–87.

[54] Hall, *Minneapolis Journal*, Apr. 13, 1896; Flandrau, *Minnesota and Tales of Frontier*, 359–60; Williams, *History of St. Paul*, 370; Folwell, *History of Minnesota*, 1: 384, 386.

[55] Henry David Thoreau, *A Week on the Concord and Merrimack Rivers* (New York: Signet Classic, 1961), 60.

[56] On culture heroes and their roles in Indian creation myths, see Thompson, *Folktale*, 305, 307–08, 310–18.

[57] [James A. Starkey], "Reminiscences of Indian Depredations: The Sunrise Expedition," *North-Western Chronotype* (St. Paul), 1 (July 1873): 50. A statue of Henry M. Rice was enshrined in Statuary Hall at the capitol in Washington, D.C., on Feb. 8, 1916; see *Minnesota History Bulletin* 1 (May 1916): 339–40.

[58] Hall, *Observations*, 50; Bruce M. White et al., comps., *Minnesota Votes: Election Returns by County for Presidents, Senators, Congressmen, and Governors, 1857–1977* (St. Paul: MHS, 1977), 153.

[59] Here and below, Hall, *Observations*, 51–52.

[60] On Rolette's celebrity status after 1857, see *St. Paul Pioneer and Democrat*, Oct. 4, 1859; Marble, "Red River," 582. His death date is reported in *St. Paul Dispatch,* Feb. 10, 1894.

of

Adele Guerin

THAT YEAR OF 1850 Adele Guerin, at the age of 24, was comfortably situated. Her husband, Vital Guerin, had built a new house for them and their five children—David, age eight, Emily, age seven, Lucy, age six, Alfred, age five, and William, age three. At the corner of Wabasha and Seventh Streets in St. Paul, their new dwelling was a one-and-a-half-story frame structure quite unlike the place that she and Vital had occupied as newly-weds on January 26, 1841. That had been a 16-by-20-foot cabin built of oak and elm logs. It had a bark roof and a puncheon floor but a real door and a window that Michel LeClaire, their neighbor, had made for them. There were only eight other cabins in St. Paul at that time.[1]

Adele had known Vital for most of her life. He had joined the American Fur Company in 1832 at the age of 19, leaving his home in Quebec for the life of a voyageur in the Upper Mississippi River region. The territory must have been to his liking, for he fulfilled his three-year contract with the company and then found work with other traders in the area. In 1839 he located on a claim in St. Paul.

Adele and her family had been among the first residents of St. Paul. She was only 10 months old when she arrived in 1827 at Fort Snelling with her parents, brother, and three sisters as refugees from the Selkirk Settlement in the Red River Valley north of Pembina. Her father, Abra-

ham Perry, had immigrated with his wife, Mary Ann, son, and two daughters from Switzerland to the Canadian wilderness in 1820. Having relocated again, they lived on a farm near the fort until 1838 when the commandant forced them off the military reserve, distressing the ladies at the fort because Adele's mother was a respected midwife. The Perrys and their neighbors had then moved downriver to a convenient landing where Pierre Parrant had already established a grog shop. All the inhabitants of this little settlement spoke French. The next year, 1839, Adele's sister Rose married James Clewett, a native of England. He had learned French when he worked as a trader for the American Fur Company; as the only one who could read and write, he had kept the books.[2]

Now St. Paul was growing rapidly. New settlers arrived almost every day on the riverboats. Just a couple of years earlier there had been only 15 families in the little village. Adele reflected on the sharp contrast with the crowds of immigrants that poured off the boats docking at the levee. There had been five hundred passengers on the *Highland Mary* alone when it docked April 19 to open the shipping season. As much as the boats and their cargoes were welcomed after the long winter, it was a mixed blessing; many of the newcomers were sick with cholera. As a mother of young children, Adele worried about their health. Even with four doctors now practicing medicine in the town, an epidemic could swiftly overtax their capacity to deal with illness.[3]

Many residents must have wondered whether there would be any shipping season on the Mississippi

Adele and Vital Guerin's new house, sketched by St. Paul pharmacist and artist Robert O. Sweeny, 1852

Water crashing over the Falls of St. Anthony, about 1855. The beginnings of Minneapolis are visible across the river.

up, however; what used to cost 10 cents now cost a quarter. While it was pleasant to have new neighbors close by, Adele sensed that her less than perfectly kept yard did not meet with the full approval of the newcomers, whose yards displayed a New England primness. Yet when she recalled the time that she and Vital could find neither a market nor a gristmill for the grain they raised and had seen it rot in the storage bin, she took comfort in the more settled and prosperous life St. Paul offered in 1850.[5]

VITAL GUERIN DIED *November 11, 1870, at the age of 58. His funeral was well attended, and the St. Paul Common Council ordered a monument for his grave.*[6]

Adele Guerin died December 20, 1914, at her home at 353 Rice Street in St. Paul. She was at that time the city's oldest woman resident. She was survived by three sons and two daughters, all residents of the St. Paul area.

—*Sarah P. Rubinstein*

River in 1850. The spring flood had been the highest ever recorded. The winter's heavy snows had been followed by equally heavy rainfall, especially in June. To make matters worse, the ice had not yet gone out when the water rose, sweeping large ice floes downriver and threatening riverbanks and the structures built on them. Adele and other St. Paul residents could hear the ice as it crashed over the Falls of St. Anthony eight miles away. Having her new house situated farther from the shore was a comfort.

Adele also reflected on her family's status in this village that was the capital of the year-old Minnesota Territory. Her husband had been one of the delegates to the Stillwater Convention in 1848 when the major work for organizing the new territory

had been carried out. He also donated land for the courthouse, which the town needed. And her brother-in-law, her sister Anne's husband Charles Bazille, had donated land for the new territorial capitol. Just recently Vital had been elected a school trustee of District Number 2, along with Joseph R. Brown and Rev. Edward D. Neill.[4]

As St. Paul grew, Adele saw it lose its French character. Most of the new immigrants came from the eastern states, founded Protestant churches, started an English-language newspaper, and taught in the English language. But a growing town had more shopping convenience to offer. She was pleased that the city market usually had fresh beef for sale, and an ice cart and a milkman now made regular rounds. The prices had gone

NOTES

[1] Here and below, J. Fletcher Williams, *A History of the City of Saint Paul to 1875* (1876; reprint, St. Paul: Minnesota Historical Society Press, 1983), 96–98, 105, 107; Patricia C. Harpole and Mary D. Nagle, eds., *Minnesota Territorial Census, 1850* (St. Paul: Minnesota Historical Society, 1972), 52.

[2] Williams, *History of St. Paul,* 101; Edward D. Neill, "Fort Snelling from 1819 to 1840," in *Minnesota Historical Society Collections* 2 (St. Paul, 1890): 137.

[3] Here and below, Williams, *History of St. Paul,* 246, 258–59, 262.

[4] Williams, *History of St. Paul,* 101, 107, 144, 182, 278–79.

[5] Williams, *History of St. Paul,* 106, 201, 265.

[6] Here and below, Williams, *History of St. Paul,* 107; *St. Paul Pioneer Press,* Dec. 21, 1914, p. 10.

Maza Okiye Win

MAY 29, 1858. MAZA OKIYE WIN (Woman Who Talks to Iron) awoke to find her grandmother leaving the tipi. Like other girls of six, she wanted to emulate her grandmother's every move, so she quickly got up to follow her. Her grandmother was already down by the banks of the Minnesota River near the Upper Sioux Agency. Realizing that she was there to offer her morning prayer, Maza Okiye Win hid behind some trees so that she would not disturb the morning devotions. She watched with interest as her grandmother stood with arms outstretched and face lifted towards the heavens, giv-ing thanks to Wakantanka, the Great Mystery. As Maza Okiye Win wit-nessed this, she hoped that, like her-self, her grandmother would pray for the safe return of her father, Chief Mazomani. He had traveled to Wash-ington, D.C., with a group of nine others from the Yellow Medicine Agency and 16 leaders from Redwood Agency to help negotiate a treaty with the United States government on behalf of the Eastern Dakota.[1]

When her grandmother finished praying, she filled her bark container with water from the river and headed back to the tipi to begin preparing their morning meal of coffee and soup left over from the previous even-ing. Before she joined her grand-mother, Maza Okiye Win rushed down to the river and splashed some of the cold, clear water on her face. She then took a big drink, said a quick prayer, and ran back to the tipi.

Today they were to begin plant-ing their Indian corn. The plum trees were blossoming, a sign that summer was coming and that it would be safe to plant without the fear of frost. Her grandmother had already taught her about the impor-tance of the corn that had been a part of their family for an untold number of generations. She had been shown the previous year how to plant four kernels in each hill and how to pray for their growth. Maza Okiye Win didn't mind this kind of work; she actually looked forward to it. She enjoyed taking an active part in the cycle of life. Besides, her mother and grandmother often used this working time to teach her about the plant relatives that would help her and others throughout life. For a girl so young, she seemed to sense that any skills she could learn would be of benefit to her in the coming years.

On this day, however, there was so much activity that it was difficult to concentrate on the task at hand and even more difficult to engage in dis-cussion. The sounds of construction were all around them. Superinten-dent Cullen and Indian Agent Brown were offering incentives such as money and goods to men who would engage in the activities of building houses and fences and who would take up the full-time cultivation of fields.[2] This, along with the addition-al pressure from missionaries and

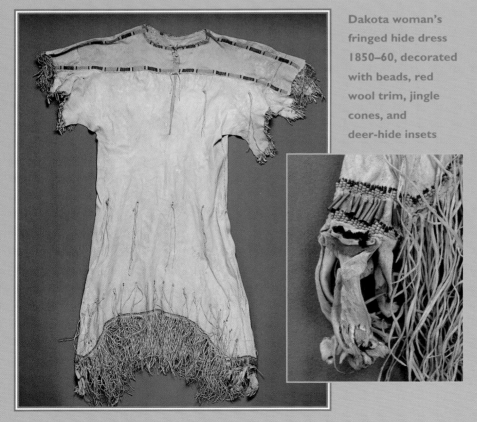

Dakota woman's fringed hide dress 1850–60, decorated with beads, red wool trim, jingle cones, and deer-hide insets

traders, meant that there were people coming and going all around them, often stopping to relate the latest changes, transactions, and building progress. Maza Okiye Win and her female relatives were absorbed in all the excitement at Upper Sioux, but they also resented the intrusion of the Dakota men into what they had always considered women's work. The whites viewed farming as men's work, but to the Dakota, planting corn had always been the occupation of the women.

Maza Okiye Win was too little to remember the last days before her father's band had moved to the reservation and could no longer go through the seasonal gathering cycle. But her other female relatives clearly missed those days and talked about them with such fondness that Maza Okiye Win missed them, too. She was having difficulty understanding why the Dakota couldn't be left alone, why all the whites were telling them that Dakota ways were wrong.

She understood that all of these issues had been weighing heavily on her father's mind before he went to Washington and that he was making the decisions he thought best. Her father had been a leader of the Wakan Wacipi (Sacred Dance or Medicine Dance), but even this had to be done in secret so that some peace could be maintained with the whites.[3] She didn't understand all the issues he faced, but she knew he was a good man and she trusted that in whatever decisions he made, he was thinking about her and her future children.

After spending all day in the fields and finishing their dinner, Maza Okiye Win and her grandmother went to check on a baby her grandmother had helped deliver the previous month. The baby, Inyangmani Hoksida (Running Walker Boy), the son of the prominent Wahpetonwan chief Inyangmani and Tawapaha Tanka Win (Her Big Hat Woman), was healthy, but it was nonetheless the practice of a good midwife to check on the mother and child for the first few months of life. Maza Okiye Win enjoyed these check-ups because they allowed her the chance to see and play with the tiny new babies. She took her job as helper very seriously and would hold the babies protectively while the mother was being examined. Little did she know that in this particular instance she was cooing over the man she would marry 27 years later.

While there, she heard some discussion among the men about the delegation in Washington. Inyangmani, a signer of the 1851 treaty, ordinarily would have been with the delegation, but, with his wife so close to delivering their son, he had not wanted to leave. The men said that rumors were spreading about the difficulty the leaders were having negotiating a treaty and the possibility that the Dakota might be left with nothing. Clearly, their lengthy stay in Washington—it had been well over two months—indicated that things were not going smoothly. Overhearing this, Maza Okiye Win began to worry whether the Dakota would ever have a place where they would be left alone or if their lands would get smaller and smaller until there was nothing.

At the age of six she was learning to cope with a constant sense of loss and the tension that comes from living in turbulent times among a nation caught between two worlds. Maza Okiye Win fell asleep that night with thoughts of her father and the uncertain future of the Dakota people.[4]

—*Angela Cavender Wilson (Tawapaha Tanka Win)*

Mazomani, photographed in Washington, D.C., 1858

NOTES

[1] Gary Clayton Anderson, *Kinsmen of Another Kind: Dakota-White Relations in the Upper Mississippi Valley, 1650–1862* (1984; reprint, St. Paul: Minnesota Historical Society Press, 1997), 228.

[2] Gary Clayton Anderson, *Little Crow: Spokesman for the Sioux* (St. Paul: Minnesota Historical Society Press, 1986), 107–08. The superintendent was William J. Cullen, the agent, Joseph R. Brown.

[3] Anderson, *Kinsmen*, 238.

[4] Much of the information presented here is based on oral accounts relayed to the author by Maza Okiye Win's descendants, particularly Elsie Cavender, Maza Okiye Win's granddaughter.

The Eden of the

H arriet E. Bishop, a young schoolteacher, moved from New England to St. Paul in 1847, two years before Minnesota Territory was formed. Despite the frontier village's crude accommodations, she was so delighted with her new home that several years later she could enthuse, "If earth has a Paradise, it is here." Another native New Englander, Ephraim S. Seymour, who toured parts of Minnesota in 1849, thought that with cultivation it would become "a perfect Eden." Later in the territorial period, the editor of the *St. Peter Courier* extolled the advantages of his Minnesota River Valley town, which he saw as "our western Eden home."[1]

Hyperbole typified the territory's boosters, who were determined to attract settlers and counteract the prevailing negative impression that their adopted home was an American

West

WILLIAM E. LASS

Siberia. Many prospective settlers perceived Minnesota as a remote, cold, desolate wilderness beyond the nation's agricultural pale. This reputation, along with the territory's vastness and sparse population, troubled Alexander Ramsey, the first territorial governor, when he presented his inaugural message to the legislature on September 4, 1849.[2]

Ramsey recognized that the extensive territory, bounded by Wisconsin on the east, Iowa on the south, the Missouri and White Earth Rivers on the west, and British possessions on the north, desperately needed settlers. A census taken in the summer of 1849 showed only 4,535 whites and mixed-bloods living in the territory of about 166,000 square miles (nearly twice the size of the later state). Other than the capital, St. Paul, the only settlements of note were

Passenger-carrying paddle-wheelers a few miles below Red Wing grace
Ferdinand Reichardt's scenic *View of the Mississippi,* 1857

Stillwater, Little Canada, St. Anthony, and the mixed-blood community of Pembina in the Red River Valley. Ramsey's address emphasized the common belief that Minnesota's future lay in agriculture. Since only about three percent of the land within its official boundaries had been acquired from the indigenous Dakota and Ojibwe who lived there, Ramsey and other promoters believed that major Indian land cessions and heavy promotional advertising were vital to the territory's rapid development.

A variety of groups and individuals—newspaper editors, guidebook authors, excursionists, organized colonies of settlers, government officials, and speculators—promoted Minnesota's acclaimed advantages. Newspapers, because of their regular distribution and relatively wide circulation outside the territory, spearheaded the promotional offensive. Setting the stage was James Madison Goodhue, the energetic editor of the *Minnesota Pioneer,* the territory's first newspaper. Launching his paper, Goodhue proclaimed that "the interests of Minnesota require an able and efficient press, to represent abroad our wants and to set forth our situation, our resources and our advantages."[3]

Until his death in August 1852, Goodhue was Minnesota's best salesman. His zealous passion for the territory's superiority was evident in his witty, colorful editorials and stories. He sometimes printed extra copies to respond to inquiries and to enable Minnesotans to mail them to acquaintances back east. He also regularly sent copies to newspapers serving areas where the most likely future Minnesotans lived—the New England, Middle Atlantic, and Old Northwest states. Oftentimes, these papers reprinted his comments verbatim, providing free advertising for Minnesota.[4]

Most other territorial newspapers used Goodhue's tactics to boast about Minnesota. John P. Owens, who successively edited three St. Paul newspapers—the *Minnesota Register,* the *Minnesota Chronicle and Register,* and the *Minnesotian*—most closely resembled Goodhue in style, dedication, and methods. Probably the single most ambitious promotion was conducted by Charles G. Ames, the editor of St. Anthony's *Minnesota Republican.* In a series of 13 articles titled "Minnesota as It Is," Ames advertised the territory's climate, natural resources, agriculture, and lumbering.[5]

NEWSPAPER BOOSTERISM was at least matched by guidebook authors John Wesley Bond, Ephraim S. Seymour, Henry W. Hamilton, Charles Emerson, A. D. Munson, and Christoper C. Andrews. Bond, a young Pennsylvanian who moved to St. Paul in 1849 and accompanied Governor Ramsey on an 1851 expedition through the

Red River Valley, wrote *Minnesota and Its Resources* in 1853 and produced updated editions in 1854, 1856, and 1857.[6] Bond masterfully mixed fact and fiction by including accurate information on such things as population and land sales along with outlandish claims for the area's uniquely salubrious climate and the superiority of its people in morality, virtue, thrift, industriousness, enterprise, and intellect.

When Seymour toured the St. Paul–St. Anthony–Stillwater area in 1849, he had already published a directory to the lead-mining region of Galena, Illinois, where he lived, and an emigrants' guide to the California gold mines.[7] By giving his book the propagandistic title *Sketches of Minnesota, the New England of the West,* Seymour suggested that the territory was a verdant, scenic area destined to be transformed into another great center of civilization. Subsequently, promoters often paid Minnesota their highest compliment by predicting it would be the country's next New England.

Bond's book, published in Chicago and Philadelphia, and Seymour's text, published in New York City, were often quoted by Minnesota and out-of-territory newspapers, and both enjoyed a wide readership. Leaders in Northampton, Massachusetts, who were organizing a colony in Minnesota specifically recommended Seymour's book to members and likely recruits.[8]

Although Henry W. Hamilton's *Rural Sketches of Minnesota, The El Dorado of the North-west,* published in Milan, Ohio, in 1850, was less widely circulated, it presented Minnesota even more favorably as a land akin to the fabled place of precious minerals sought by Spanish explorers. To Hamilton, Minnesota was a preferred alternative to California, which was being grandly promoted as the "New El Dorado" after the 1849 gold rush.

A. D. Munson's *The Minnesota Messenger Containing Sketches of the Rise and Progress of Minnesota* and Charles L. Emerson's *Rise and Progress of Minnesota Territory* were both published in St. Paul in 1855 while the city and territory were experiencing unprecedented growth. Munson reiterated the standard claims that Minnesota was a haven for health seekers, and Emerson's booklet, originally issued in October 1854 in the *Minnesota Democrat* when Emerson was its editor, emphasized St. Paul's vibrant economy.

Christopher C. Andrews's *Minnesota and Dacotah,* published in Washington, D.C., in 1857, was the territory's last promotional book. Based on a series of popular letters Andrews sent to the *Boston Post* while touring Minnesota in 1856, it was not as overdone as some of the other books, but it nonetheless could have caused eager land seekers to imagine Minnnesota as the Garden of Eden.

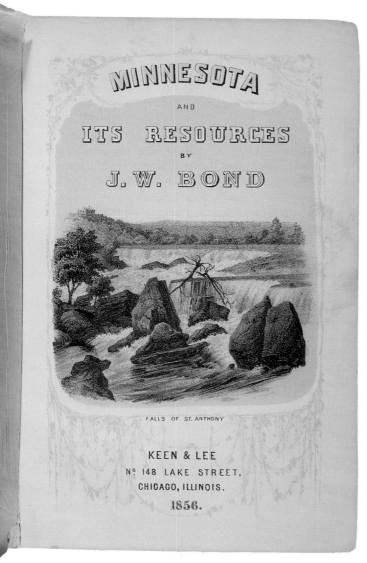

MINNESOTA

AND

ITS RESOURCES

BY

J. W. BOND

FALLS OF ST. ANTHONY

KEEN & LEE
Nº 148 LAKE STREET,
CHICAGO, ILLINOIS.
1856.

Title page of the 1856 edition of John Wesley Bond's early book promoting Minnesota

THOUSANDS OF TOURISTS also helped publicize the territory. Typically they booked steamboat tours from St. Louis or Galena to St. Paul, the base for visiting sites such as the Falls of St. Anthony, Minnehaha Falls, and Fort Snelling. The "Fashionable Tour," as it came to be known, was first proposed in 1835 by artist George Catlin, who aptly sensed the appeal of the Mississippi River's scenic attractions to well-to-do American and foreign travelers. By the late 1830s excursion tours originating in St. Louis had become popular, and the number of these fashionable excursions increased after accommodations in St. Paul improved.[9]

Two of the best-known steamboat excursionists in the early territorial years were women. The Swedish novelist Fredrika Bremer, her international reputation already well established, visited St. Paul and its environs in October 1850, a year after beginning her lengthy tour of the United States.[10]

Recognizing Bremer's promotional potential, Governor Ramsey and his wife Anna hosted the celebrity during her eight-day stay, and they must have felt gratified when her *Homes of the New World,* published in 1853, praised Minnesota's agricultural potential and prophetically observed,

> This Minnesota is a glorious country, and just the country for Northern emigrants. . . . It is four times as large as England; its soil is of the richest description, with extensive wooded tracts; great numbers of rivers and lakes abounding in fish, and a healthy, invigorating climate. . . . What a glorious new Scandinavia might not Minnesota become![11]

American writer Elizabeth Ellet made a trip in 1852 that became even more widely known than Bremer's. A frequent contributor to national magazines such as *Godey's Lady's Book,* Ellet gloried in Minnesota's scenery and described Minnehaha Falls as a "vision of beauty" that formed "a scene of such enchanting loveliness as to take the senses captive, and steep the soul in the purest enjoyment this earth can afford." Her travelogue, first printed serially in the New York *Daily Tribune* in August and September 1852, was excerpted by other newspapers including the *St. Anthony Express.* Her book *Summer Rambles in the West,* published the next year, included extensive coverage of Minnesota's scenic attractions and promoted fashionable tours.[12]

The single greatest promotional act of the territorial period was the Rock Island Railroad Excursion of 1854. Upon reaching the Mississippi at Rock Island, Illinois, on February 22, the Chicago and Rock Island Railroad celebrated by organizing an excursion to the head of navigation. Invited were hundreds of celebrities including politicians such as former president Millard Fillmore, businessmen, academicians, and journalists from most major eastern newspapers and cities such as Chicago and Cincinnati.[13]

The three-day tour proved so popular that its organizers had to employ five very crowded steamboats to carry the 1,200 excursionists to St. Paul that June. During their one very long day in Minnesota, coaches and every other conceivable vehicle whisked them to the Falls of St. Anthony, Lake Calhoun, Minnehaha Falls, and Fort Snelling. After a grand reception at the St. Paul capitol hosted by Governor Willis A. Gorman,

Fashionable visitors admiring Minnehaha Falls, front and back

by nationally known writer Catherine M. Sedgwick, was published in *Putnam's Monthly Magazine* of September 1854. But dozens of other stories about the scenic upper Mississippi appeared in newspapers. While river tourists did not have an opportunity to become well acquainted with the interior of Minnesota, they did see the verdant river valley during the summer, which stimulated comparisons to New England. For example, Charles F. Babcock, editor of the New Haven *Palladium,* thought that the scenery at St. Paul and St. Anthony was "not unlike that observed in some of the drives around New Haven." As a result of the great excursion, Christopher C. Andrews reported, a remarkable 28,000 people visited St. Paul during the 1856 navigation season.[14]

LEADERS OF ORGANIZED settlement colonies became some of Minnesota's most enthusiastic promoters. They typically formed organizations with a formal name, bylaws, and membership dues. Colonies were touted as superior to individual settlement because advance agents could preselect land claims and often handle the legal requirements of obtaining titles. Once established, the group could cooperatively build homes, schools, and churches.

Members of each colony often shared a unifying trait. The Minnesota Claim Association, for example, was usually called the Northampton Colony after the Massachusetts city where it was organized. Headed by Methodist clergymen Freeman Nutting and Henry Martyn Nichols and extensively publicized for several months in the *Northampton Courier* and by exchanges with other eastern newspapers, the organization sent settlers to Chanhassen, Faribault, and St. Peter in 1853. The Minnesota Settlement Association of New York City concentrated on city folk in its 1855 advertising blitz in the *New York Daily Tribune,* and by spring 1856 it had garnered an impressive 250 members who prepared to move.[15]

A territorial official played a strong hand in Minnesota's most unique colony and definitely its greatest failure. The Western Farm and Village Association of New York City represented a group of urban, working-class members. Inspired by the physiocratic tradition of the naturalness of the yeoman farmer and, apparently, various utopian settlements, the association disparaged the wage system in favor of agriculture. The decision to move to Winona County in 1852 was in part a response to Henry H. Sibley, territorial delegate to Congress.[16]

Through his pamphlet, *Minnesota Territory: Its Present Condition and Prospects,* and in correspondence with the association, Sibley glorified the prospects of living the good life in rural Minnesota. He even introduced a proposal in the House of Representatives to grant 160 acres

the visitors departed just before midnight. Speaking at the reception, Fillmore lauded in terms of just praise the scenery and prospects of the country and expatiated at length on its beauty and resources. A newspaper account continued, "He spoke of the adaptation of St. Paul as a summer place of fashionable resort, and believed it would eventually be connected in an unbroken chain of railway with the Atlantic and Pacific Oceans. He should go home with enlarged ideas of the future greatness of Minnesota." Quite likely he had been made aware that local boosters were predicting greatness for the city because of its central location in the continent.

Perhaps the most widely circulated article about the trip, "The Great Excursion to the Falls of St. Anthony" of federal land to each association member. Despite the failure of this private homestead bill, about 175 colony members moved to Rolling Stone in Winona County in 1852. While their cause seemed noble, they were stunningly naive about the realities of frontier life. Disease, a high death rate, poor land selection, bad roads, and lack of supplies forced most of the colonists, including the chief organizer, to leave Rolling Stone within a few months.

OTHER OFFICIALS WHO actively promoted Minnesota included Alexander Ramsey and Willis A. Gorman. Ramsey skillfully used his annual messages to the legislature to praise Minnesota's climate, healthfulness, agricultural potential, and future greatness. His words were

Splendid cabin of the steamboat *Milwaukee* (right) and the steamers *Grey Eagle, Frank Steele, Jeannette Roberts,* and *Time and Tide* at St. Paul's lower levee, 1859

distributed generously by Minnesota newspapers and such national business magazines as *De Bow's Review.*

Ramsey also promoted the territory officially in order to more effectively compete with Wisconsin and other states that were using public funds and government employees to advertise for settlers. Ramsey and the legislature were persuaded by William G. Le Duc to sponsor a Minnesota exhibit at the 1853 Crystal Palace world's fair in New York City. As the appointed fair commissioner, Le Duc, an irregular correspondent for Horace Greeley's *New York Tribune* and the publisher of the somewhat promotional annual titled *The Minnesota Year Book,* was granted $300 to display Minnesota products.[17]

As a result of his New York experience, Le Duc recommended that Minnesota should officially begin recruiting foreigners for settlement. The 1854 legislature considered that possibility but did not act. Ramsey's successor, however, Willis A. Gorman, strongly urged official promotion. Responding to his call, the 1855 legislature created the position of Commissioner of Emigration, and Gorman then named Eugene Burnand, a Swiss immigrant who had recruited Europeans in New York, to the position.[18]

As specified in the authorizing legislation, Burnand established his headquarters in New York City where he could best meet European immigrants and interest them in Minnesota. During his two-year tenure, he also advertised the territory in European newspapers and corresponded with groups of immigrants who had recently moved to other American cities. Concentrating on Germans, Burnand successfully persuaded many of them, including the Cincinnati German Association, which played a key role in founding New Ulm, to move to Minnesota.

While serving as territorial delegate, Sibley made his first promotional effort in a February 15, 1850, letter to U.S. Senator Henry S. Foote of Mississippi. Portraying Minnesota in glowing terms, the letter, first printed in the Washington, D.C., *Union,*

became the core of Sibley's promotional pamphlet *Minnesota Territory: Its Present Condition and Prospects,* printed by the Washington *Globe* on February 20, 1852. With slight changes it was again published in the *Daily National Intelligencer* (Washington) on November 5, 1852, and in some Minnesota newspapers.[19]

LAND SPECULATORS REPRESENTED a last important source of territorial promotion. Although the press regularly vilified them as greedy vultures who preyed on a vulnerable populace, speculators were not solely big-monied investors. In truth, during the heady boom times before the devastating Panic of 1857, speculation permeated all segments of Minnesota society. Johann Georg Kohl, a German geographer who visited Minnesota in 1855, observed that "in St. Paul, every shoemaker, every laborer, every maid, and every stableboy, whoever has saved money, dreams and fantasizes about a hole, a rock, a swamp, a thornbush, a piece of land or (as they say here) a *lot* outside the city somewhere." [20]

Speculators and their allies came in many guises, including colonists, land-company agents, townsite promoters, community boosters, and ordinary citizens. Using a pseudonym such as "Northwest," "Benton," or

A hand-crafted wooden immigrant's trunk from Norway, 1850s

"T." to send letters to Minnesota and out-of-state newspapers about the special qualities of their communities, they praised the territory's farmland, crops, timber, mill sites, and destiny of becoming a regional metropolis. Quite likely these authors were disguised agents for land companies, but some may have been nothing more than another "Mr. Everyman," whose own investment depended on the success of his town. Interestingly, by the mid-1850s boom, the existence of speculation was itself promoted as one of Minnesota's great attractions, and stories of land values doubling or tripling in a few months became commonplace.[21]

MINNESOTA'S SUPPOSEDLY UNIQUE climate represented a challenge for promoters. Collectively defensive, they resented any critical comments or inferences that Minnesota was a Siberia, a second Lapland, a polar region, or too far north for productive agriculture. Gorman complained, for instance, that "during the past year I have received almost innumerable letters from the middle states propounding a variety of questions about our territory, especially desiring to know if our winters are not very long, and so exceedingly cold that stock freezes to death, and man hardly dare venture out of his domicil." Likewise, Burnand complained about agents from some states, whom he claimed frightened emigrants from risking their lives "among the alledged [*sic*] *mountains of ice* in this Territory."[22]

Minnesota's spokesmen went to the opposite extreme by presenting its climate as the world's best. Like their critics, they assumed the ridiculous posture that climate conformed to political boundaries and, thus, that Minnesota somehow had a climate distinctive even from neighboring Iowa and Wisconsin. Most of their verbiage was devoted to the winter season because it was Minnesota's bugbear. They described winters as dry, clear, calm, devoid of sharp temperature fluctuations, and invigorating. While newspaper editors and other boosters sometimes presented winter-weather statistics, promoters preferred "bracing" as their favorite synonym for cold. Summaries of winter weather usually included commentary that a really cold day was not really cold because people did not feel it to the extent they did in more humid climates to the east and south.[23]

On a philosophical plane, promoters contended that Minnesota's climate in fact assured its future greatness. Their proof was the geopolitical notion that the world's great civilizations had developed in temperate climatic zones. Editor Goodhue, for example, informed his readers that "the human family, never has accomplished anything worthy of note, beside the erection of pyramids, those milestones of ancient centuries, south

A horse-drawn sleigh waits in front of a busy St. Anthony land office in this 1/4-plate daguerreotype, about 1857.

of latitude 40 degrees north. The history of the *world,* is written chiefly above that parallel."[24]

Specifically relating that concept to Minnesota, an expansive writer for *De Bow's Review* claimed:

> There seems to be a certain zone of climate within which humanity reaches the highest degree of physical and mental power. . . . That zone, rizing northward by some immutable law of nature, brought out from the Saxon family all its decided features of character. . . . That zone struck this country where the pilgrim and the Quaker landed, and has ever since been streaming across the continent in one unbroken path of progress and glory. . . . It is the good fortune of this Territory to lie not only within that zone, but within its very apex.[25]

Such observations, which later seemed quaint, if not ludicrous, were perfectly reasonable to those smitten with the nationalistic fervor of Manifest Destiny. Ramsey expressed the same sentiment when he declared that there was no movement of people

> recorded in the annals of the world, that does not sink in comparison by side of that marvellous American progress, that astonishing growth and development of our triumphant, irresistible civilization, which in its

march to the uttermost extremities of the West, has passed the barrier of the Alleghanies[sic], peopled the valley of the Mississippi, crossed the Rocky Mountains, and planted our glorious liberty and benign institutions by the shores of the Pacific.[26]

Promoters found a strong correlation between Minnesota's winters and the sterling character of its people. They held that the long winters stimulated industriousness, frugality, inquisitiveness, enterprise, and intellect. Their reasoning was that Minnesotans had to work hard during the growing season to prepare for winter, which in turn was a time of contemplation, winter sports, and socializing to share ideas. In assessing the nature of Minnesotans, Bond observed:

I speak in no boastful or vainglorious theme when I say there is largely more *character* in Minnesota than was found at the same age in any of the older western members of our republican family. I know the fact from the experience of candid men, who have lived on other frontiers, and now bear testimony in favor of Minnesota. Croakers and grumblers we may ever expect to find among us—drones and loafers; but the great family of the hive works together steadily and harmoniously. They, and those who are to come after them, will reap their reward in a glorious, happy, and enviable future.[27]

The most extravagant claim about Minnesota's climate was that it was salubrious. In addressing the first territorial legislature, Ramsey stated that the "Northern latitude saves us from the malaria and death, which in other climes are so often attendant upon a liberal soil." Sibley boldly proclaimed that in Minnesota "sickness has no dwelling place," and in the same vein Goodhue declared that "never has a case of fever and ague originated here." Such claims prompted some Minnesotans to joke that in order to die they would have to leave the territory.[28]

In territorial years there was a certain plausibility to these extreme assertions. Until the mid-1870s the American public, including the medical profession, believed that climatic features were primary causes of disease, and, hence, they accepted the premise of healthy and unhealthy climates. Americans also knew that newly opened areas often were ravaged by diseases.[29] Naturally preoccupied with their own health, it is not too surprising that some might have believed that somewhere on the globe there was a magnificent, salubrious climate. Coincidentally, the formation of Minnesota Territory and a great cholera epidemic occurred within several months of each other.

Introduced from western Europe, a strain of Asiatic cholera had devastated settled areas of the United States in 1832. Abating for 17 years, it resurfaced in 1849, causing a national health crisis. New York City had 5,017 cholera fatalities in a three-month period, and the disease killed a tenth of the people in St. Louis. The calamity moved President Zachary Taylor to proclaim Friday, August 3, 1849, a national day of "fasting, humiliation and prayer" to implore the Almighty to lift the pestilence from the land.[30]

Since cholera was especially prevalent in filthy, crowded cities with garbage heaps, uncollected animal waste, and contaminated water, Minnesota escaped it in 1849. This absence, which was errantly attributed to the salubrious climate, gave credence to the territory's promotional claims. But when cholera reappeared nationally in 1854 and 1855, Minnesota was not so fortunate. At least a dozen St. Paulites died from it in 1854, but city promoters took steps to preserve the territory's reputation for healthiness. Receiving a report from the board of health about the cholera outbreak, the city council squelched the information. Council minutes did not mention the report, and city newspapers ignored it. Although cases probably increased in 1855, St. Paul's newspapers only mentioned it twice.[31]

Malaria or ague was perhaps the most dreaded disease in much of the nation. Especially prevalent in hot regions, it was believed to be caused by miasma, a vapor arising from warm-water swamps. Without knowledge that malaria (a word contracted from the Italian *mala aria* or bad air) was transmitted by only certain types of mosquitoes, Minnesota's promoters bragged that its absence was attributable to the territory's good air. For example, Bond assured his readers that after several years' residency in Minnesota, "I can safely say that the atmosphere is more pure, pleasant, and healthful, than that of any other I have ever breathed on the continent of North or South America."[32]

From time to time during the territorial period, Minnesota's promoters changed the emphasis of their health claims. References to cholera became uncommon after the 1849 epidemic, and comments on malaria were expanded to include any ailments associated with fevers. By later territorial years consumption had become the disease for which Minnesota's cool climate frequently was claimed to be an elixir.

The proof for claims of bringing good health was only anecdotal. Sometimes individuals testified that the climate had improved or even cured them. Promoter Hamilton cited the case of an acquaintance from Ohio who "was thought to be consumptive and having heard much about this bracing and invigorating climate, he thought he would try it, and see what effect it would have upon his lungs. His health gradually improved, and before the following spring he was well and hearty, with an appetite like a Turk." John H. Stevens, later famed as a founder of Minneapolis, was consumptive when he moved west in 1848. He wrote that his small Wisconsin party included a doctor, but after they arrived in Minnesota, "There were no sick—the doctor left in disgust." In describing the area north of Stillwater, Seymour observed: "The healthiness of this place can not be questioned. A single death by sickness has not occurred among the white population within the last year. The only death was that of a young man, killed by the falling of a tree."[33]

MINNESOTA PUBLICISTS also promoted the territory's potential for agriculture, playing on the popular American metaphor of the frontier as a future garden—a paradise created without travail by yeoman farmers. Waxing enthusiastic about the St. Paul–Stillwater area, Seymour predicted that "it will, ere long, be dotted with farmhouses, and enlivened with the songs of multitudes of cheerful and thriving husbandmen." After the Dakota cession treaties of 1851, promoters turned to the region along the Minnesota River and its tributaries. Ramsey himself declared it to be "the garden spot of Minnesota."[34]

Much agricultural promotion sought to convince farmers that the territory was not too far north to raise the usual eastern crops. Consequently, a favorite ploy was to emphasize Minnesota's centrality—not its northness. Promoters accurately pointed out that St. Paul was on the same latitude as southern France and northern Italy and well to the south of Great Britain and Germany. Ramsey told of successful farming north of even northernmost Minnesota. After seeing extensive cultivated fields at the juncture of the Red and Assiniboine Rivers (present-day Winnipeg, Manitoba), he pronounced that area "a picture of rural affluence and comfort."[35] Ramsey's inferential

proof that all of Minnesota was potentially farmland was often repeated by other promoters.

Although only a small portion of Minnesota was cultivated during the territorial years, promoters did not hesitate to boast about the productivity of its rich soils. Other advantages such as cheap land, nearby markets for farm produce at lumbering camps and Indian agencies, and accessibility to timber and water were also held out as inducements to prospective settlers.[36]

Emphasizing climate, health, and agriculture, promoters also praised Minnesota's water transportation, waterpower, lumbering, scenery, and outdoor sports. In the prerailroad age, navigable waterways were a major concern, and Minnesota's growth seemed assured because of its location at the head of the Mississippi River and Great Lakes commercial arteries. During the early territorial period, the Missouri River was prominently mentioned, but this stopped as the boundaries of the future state became evident. Promoters had a knack for making all of the Mississippi's northern

Daguerreotype showing St. Anthony Falls, whose waterpower was quickly harnessed for milling lumber, and the new businesses on St. Anthony's Main Street, about 1855

tributaries appear to be navigable, conveying the message that steamboats could service the farming frontier.

Comments on waterpower elicited the usual comparisons to New England's industrial cities, and, thus, the Falls of St. Anthony reinforced the contention that Minnesota was the New England of the West. Promoters only vaguely sensed the extent of Minnesota's pineries and had absolutely no perspective on their future exploitation, so they simply called them "inexhaustible."[37] Descriptions of the beautiful scenery concentrated on the Mississippi River and on lakes in timbered areas.

Booming settlement in 1855–56 prompted promoters to stress rapid development as one of Minnesota's greatest attractions. Well aware of the common assumption that frontiers were backward, they advertised Minnesota's growth to show that it was indeed "civilized." In noting rapid change in St. Paul, which had an estimated population of 10,000 in 1856, Andrews observed:

As I stood looking at the city, I recalled the picture in Mr. Bond's work, and contrasted its present with the

appearance it had three or four years ago. What a change! Three or four steamers were lying at the levee; steam and smoke were shooting forth from the chimneys of numerous manufactories; a ferry was plying the Mississippi, transporting teams and people; church steeples and domes and great warehouses stood in places which were vacant as if but yesterday; busy streets had been built and peopled; rows of splendid dwellings and villas, adorned with delightful terraces and gardens, had been erected.[38]

Promoters proved no exception to the principle that those who love one place tend to disparage others. In portraying Minnesota as exceptionally desirable, they derided New England's soil as rocky, churlish, and exhausted. They found the climates of the Middle Atlantic states and Ohio River valley too damp and unhealthy, the southern slave states enervating, sickly, and unproductive. The routine, caustic lambasting of the South evidenced the spirit of self-assumed Yankee superiority, reflecting many of the promoters' Yankee ancestry and

Bustling St. Paul, a detail of B. F. Upton's panorama taken just before the panic of 1857 slowed growth; in the foreground are workmen laying bricks for a new county jail at Cedar and Fifth Streets; in the background is the Methodist-Episcopal church at Jackson and Ninth Streets.

the certitude of their Puritan forefathers. Even those of non-Yankee genesis adopted the Yankee value system. Often, the slaveholding South was expanded conceptually into a Greater South, including even Illinois and southern Iowa, that was then criticized for its "ague producing" lands. By 1856 the slavery conflict in "Bleeding Kansas" and Indian troubles in Oregon and Washington territories provided another opportunity to show Minnesota's superiority. California, growing rampantly because of its gold rush, was an object of particular scorn. Promoters derided it as a lawless, immoral Sodom and Gomorrah lacking the elements that assured future greatness.[39]

Minnesota's publicists made contributions in addition to attracting settlers to the territory. They set the stage for the revival of state-sponsored promotion and the continuation of private promotion throughout the frontier farming period. Their emphasis on salubrious Minnesota was continued until the 1880s, and by attracting thousands of sick people to Minnesota, they planted the seeds of the state's vigorous public-health program. Their predictions about Minnesota's future greatness not only seemed to provide moral justification for Indian land cessions, but stimulated Minnesota's later Manifest Destiny demands for annexing central Canada. The elitist promotional descriptions of the moral and intellectual superiority of Minnesotans was a precursor of Social Darwinism, which, among other things, emphasized the superiority of white people.[40]

Lastly, by defining the nature of Minnesota they provided a common identity to the new people called Minnesotans. As portrayed by promoters, Minnesotans were industrious, frugal, practical, intelligent, moral, very defensive about their climate and cultural attainments, and proud of their new home. Present-day Minnesotans should have no difficulty recognizing familiar elements of their image that date to these territorial years. 🦌

NOTES

[1] *Weekly Minnesotian* (St. Paul), Nov. 5, 1853; E. S. Seymour, *Sketches of Minnesota, the New England of the West* (New York: Harper, 1850), 118; *St. Peter Courier,* Aug. 20, 1856.

[2] Here and below, William E. Lass, "Minnesota: An American Siberia?" *Minnesota History* 49 (Winter 1984): 149; Minnesota Territory, *Journal of the Council,* 1849, p. 95–97; William W. Folwell, *A History of Minnesota* (St. Paul, Minnesota Historical Society [MHS], 1956), 1: 253, 352.

[3] *Minnesota Pioneer* (St. Paul), Apr. 28, 1849.

[4] Mary W. Berthel, *Horns of Thunder: The Life and Times of James M. Goodhue including Selections from His Writings* (St. Paul: MHS, 1948), 76, 260.

[5] George S. Hage, *Newspapers on the Minnesota Frontier, 1849–1860* (St. Paul: MHS, 1967), 16; Daniel S. B. Johnston, "Minnesota Journalism in the Territorial Period," in *Minnesota Historical Society Collections* 10 (St. Paul, 1905): 255; *Minnesota Republican* (St. Anthony), Feb. 22–July 26, 1855.

[6] *National Union Catalog: Pre-1956 Imprints* (London: Mansell, 1970), 65: 427.

[7] *Union Catalog,* 540: 244.

[8] *Weekly Minnesotian,* Feb. 5, 1853.

[9] Theodore C. Blegen, "The 'Fashionable Tour' on the Upper Mississippi," *Minnesota History* 20 (Dec. 1939): 379, 383.

[10] John T. Flanagan, "Fredrika Bremer: Traveler and Prophet," *Minnesota History* 20 (June 1939): 130–37.

[11] Fredrika Bremer, *Homes of the New World,* trans. by Mary Howitt (New York: Harper, 1853), 2: 55–56.

[12] Elizabeth Ellet, *Summer Rambles in the West* (New York: J. C. Riker, 1853), 101; [Henry A. Bright], *Happy Country This America: The Travel Diary of Henry Arthur Bright* (Columbus: Ohio State University Press, 1978), 276n; *St. Anthony Express,* Aug. 20, 1852.

[13] Here and below, William J. Petersen, "The Rock Island Railroad Excursion of 1854," *Minnesota History* 15 (Dec. 1934): 405–15; *Daily Pioneer,* June 10, 1854.

[14] Sedgwick reprinted as Bertha L. Heilbron, ed., "By Rail and River to Minnesota in 1854," *Minnesota History* 25 (June 1944): 103–16; Charles F. Babcock, "Rails West: The Rock Island Excursion of 1854," *Minnesota History* 34 (Winter 1954): 140; C. C. Andrews, *Minnesota and Dacotah* (Washington: R. Farnham, 1857), 38.

[15] See *Northampton Courier,* Sept. 28, Oct. 26, Nov. 30, 1852, Apr. 26, 1853, in *Northampton Courier* extracts of Minnesota-interest collection, MHS, and these articles by Charles W. Nichols: "Henry Martyn Nichols and the Northampton Colony," "The Northampton Colony and Chanhassen," and, "New Light on the Northampton Colony," in *Minnesota History* 19 (June 1938): 129–47, 20 (June 1939): 140–45, and 22 (June 1941): 169–73. See also *New York Daily Tribune,* Sept. 26, 1855, Apr. 9, 1856, in *New York Tribune* extracts of Minnesota-interest collection, MHS.

[16] Here and below, Christopher M. Johnson, "The Rolling Stone Colony: Labor Rhetoric in Action," *Minnesota History* 49 (Winter 1984): 140–48.

[17] William G. Le Duc, "Minnesota at the Crystal Palace Exhibition, New York, 1853," *Minnesota History Bulletin* 1 (Aug. 1916): 352, 364. Wisconsin had a commissioner of emigration from 1852 to 1854 and resumed official promotion in 1867. Iowa did not have full-fledged official promotion until 1870. See Theodore C. Blegen, "The Competition of the Northwestern States for Immigrants," *Wisconsin Magazine of History* 3 (Sept. 1919): 4–11.

[18] Here and below, Livia Appel and Theodore C. Blegen,

eds., "Official Encouragement of Immigration to Minnesota during the Territorial Period," *Minnesota History Bulletin* 5 (Aug. 1923): 170, 172, 193, 201.

[19] For letter to Foote, see Sibley, "Description of Minnesota," in *Minnesota Historical Society Collections* 1 (St. Paul, 1872): 37–42; copies of Sibley's pamphlet and the *Intelligencer* article are in MHS. Sibley's letter to Foote and his circular were also published in the *St. Anthony Express*, Feb. 7, Apr. 3, 1852, respectively.

[20] "Johann Georg Kohl: A German Traveler in Minnesota Territory," trans. and ed. by Frederic Trautmann, *Minnesota History* 49 (Winter 1984): 131.

[21] For examples of community promotion and the beneficial effects of speculation, see Andrews, *Minnesota and Dacotah,* 131; *Minnesota Republican,* June 28, 1855; *Minnesota Weekly Times* (St. Paul), July 26, Aug. 23, 1856; *St. Anthony Express,* Aug. 27, 1852; *St. Peter Courier,* Aug. 20, 1856; *Weekly Minnesotian,* Dec. 13, 1851, July 30, Nov. 26, 1853, June 28, 1856; *Winona Republican,* Aug. 12, 1856.

[22] Minnesota Territory, *Journal of the Council,* 1855, p. 32; Appel and Blegen, "Official Encouragement of Immigration," 194.

[23] See especially J. Wesley Bond, *Minnesota and Its Resources* (Philadelphia: Charles Desilver, 1857), 63–69; Charles L. Emerson, *Rise and Progress of Minnesota Territory* (St. Paul: C. L. Emerson, 1855), 2; A. D. Munson, ed., *The Minnesota Messenger Containing Sketches of the Rise and Progress of Minnesota* (St. Paul: A. D. Munson, 1855), 13; *Minnesota Chronicle and Register,* Feb. 23, 1850; *Minnesota Republican,* Mar. 1, 1855.

[24] *Minnesota Pioneer,* Sept. 26, 1850.

[25] *De Bow's Review* (Washington, D.C.), 21 (July 1856): 72.

[26] Minnesota Territory, *Journal of the Council,* 1851, p. 11.

[27] Bond, *Minnesota and Its Resources,* 24.

[28] Minnesota Territory, *Journal of the Council,* 1849, p. 7; Sibley, "Description of Minnesota," 42; *Minnesota Pioneer,* June 5, 1851; *Northampton Courier,* July 1, 1856.

[29] Philip D. Jordan, *The People's Health: A History of Public Health in Minnesota* (St. Paul: MHS, 1953), 1–4; Madge E. Pickard and R. Carlyle Buley, *The Midwest Pioneer: His Ills, Cures & Doctors* (New York: R. E. Banta, 1945), 9–14.

[30] Charles E. Rosenberg, *The Cholera Years: The United States in 1832, 1849, and 1866* (Chicago: University of Chicago Press, 1962), 36–39, 114–15, 121–22, 145. For all of Taylor's proclamation, see *Minnesota Pioneer,* Aug. 2, 1849.

[31] John M. Armstrong, "The Asiatic Cholera in St. Paul," *Minnesota History* 14 (Sept. 1933): 288, 292, 295.

[32] Lass, "Minnesota: An American Siberia?" 152; Bond, *Minnesota and Its Resources,* 64.

[33] H. S. Hamilton, *Rural Sketches of Minnesota, the El Dorado of the North-west* (Milan, Oh.: Waggoner, 1850), 10; Munson, *Minnesota Messenger,* 53; Seymour, *Sketches of Minnesota,* 206.

[34] Seymour, *Sketches of Minnesota,* 179; Minnesota Territory, *Journal of the Council,* 1852, p. 25. For extensive discussion of the garden image, see Henry Nash Smith, *Virgin Land: The American West as Symbol and Myth* (Cambridge, Mass.: Harvard University Press, 1950).

[35] Minnesota Territory, *Journal of the Council,* 1852, p. 27.

[36] Here and below, Bond, *Minnesota and Its Resources,* 103; *Minnesota Chronicle and Register,* Feb. 23, 1850; *Minnesota Democrat,* Apr. 20, 1853; *Minnesota Republican,* Mar. 22, 1855; Seymour, *Sketches of Minnesota,* 125, 205, 265.

[37] Andrews, *Minnesota and Dacotah,* 87; Bond, *Minnesota and Its Resources,* 20; *Minnesota Pioneer,* Apr. 8, 1852.

[38] Andrews, *Minnesota and Dacotah,* 36–37.

[39] *Winona Republican,* Aug. 12, 1856; Andrews, *Minnesota and Dacotah,* 87, 116; Bond, *Minnesota and Its Resources,* 22, 162; *Minnesota Pioneer,* June 7, 1849, June 5, 1851.

[40] For promotion efforts after statehood, see Peter J. Ristuben, *Minnesota and the Competition for Immigrants* (Ann Arbor: University Microfilms, 1964). For Minnesota's appeal to health seekers, see Helen Clapesattle, "When Minnesota Was Florida's Rival," *Minnesota History* 35 (Mar. 1957): 214–21. For the long-range effects of Minnesota's recruitment of consumptives, see J. Arthur Myers, *Invited and Conquered: Historical Sketch of Tuberculosis in Minnesota* (St. Paul: Minnesota Public Health Association, 1949). On Minnesota's manifest-destiny campaign, see Alvin C. Gluek Jr., *Minnesota and the Manifest Destiny of the Canadian Northwest: A Study in Canadian-American Relations* (Toronto: University of Toronto Press, 1965).

A DAY IN THE LIFE
of
Cecelia O'Brien

FRIDAY, SEPTEMBER 27, 1850, and Cecelia O'Brien was daydreaming again. There were clothes to wash, dry, and get ready for the ironing tomorrow, but the work hardly relieved her boredom. Here at Fort Snelling one day was like another. She stared at the light glaring in through the high basement window and listened idly to Mrs. Kirkham's footsteps and the cries of the baby coming from upstairs.

Kate Kirkham, the well-bred wife of Capt. Ralph W. Kirkham, had taken in Cecelia as a laundress and mother's helper a few months before. Not that the girl was orphaned or destitute. Cecelia's mother, Catharine, lived and worked just across the river in Mr. Sibley's fine stone house in Mendota. But Catharine had decided that when Cecelia turned 13 she would have to earn some money, so she rented out her daughter for a few dollars a month. The captain had at first objected—the army only gave him $5 a month to pay for domestic help, and he had to foot the bill for any extra.[1]

Cecelia had looked forward to the change. Truth to tell, she'd been more than a little frightened by all of the Indians and rough French-speaking characters in Mendota. And surely life in that castle high up on the bluff would be exciting. The accommodations—a shared bed in the cellar kitchen of an officer's apartment—couldn't be any worse than what Cecelia had known since she was born. Best of all, she had heard—correctly, it turned out—that many of the soldiers there hailed from Ireland, as she did.

Mendota as seen from Fort Snelling; Henry Sibley's two-story stone house is at center. Sgt. Edward K. Thomas painted this oil, *Fort Snelling*, in about 1850 while stationed there.

But the soldiers paid little attention to her and seemed to be as bored with the routine in the garrison as she was in the Kirkhams' basement. Laundry, even for a small household, meant hauling and boiling water, keeping a fire going in the wood stove, scrubbing, wringing, drying, and—worst of all—ironing, that back-breaker of a Saturday chore, squeezed in between bread-baking duties. At least baby Julia's soiled clouts did not have to be ironed, but everything else did. She had always thought of herself as stronger and more grown-up than other girls—her father had always said so—but now she just felt tired. Except for the occasional sewing lesson or a Sunday in Mendota with her mother, her days were broken only by daydreaming and memories.

"In old Ireland, every man was a soldier." Cecelia's father's words came back to her often. He'd been anxious to get out of the king's army—just another way for the English to grind down the Irish, he had said—and get to America to sign on with the U.S. Army, where an Irishman could be a hero. He was consumed by the idea, reading what little he could find about America and the war with Mexico. When he read about the triumphs of an American army officer named O'Brien—well, that sealed it. Brushing aside the scoffs of his wife, he immediately made plans to emigrate. It was high time to leave: Black '47, a year of legendary cold and snow, famine and horror. But he never made it to his American dream, dying at sea and leaving Cecelia and Catharine to fend for themselves.[2]

Catharine O'Brien could have stayed in Boston where she and her daughter had landed late in 1847. The demand there for servant girls was high, since no one but an Irish immigrant woman was willing to work in a degrading state of servility in someone else's home. Pay for servant girls was about $5 a month, but Catharine assumed it would be even higher in a frontier boom town. So she and Cecelia made their way to raw, bountiful Minnesota Territory, a place where even an Irish widow pushing 40 could make a living.[3]

They had landed in St. Paul on the first steamboat of the season—on April 19, 1850—along with 500 other eager immigrants. Knee-deep waters from a heavy spring flood filled the streets and some of the warehouses along the levee. Just about every building was made of wood, and all looked like they'd been built a day or two before. Catharine and Cecelia felt lucky to find some space in a still-unfinished boardinghouse in this town that seemed to be bursting its brand-new seams. What most amazed them were all the different kinds of people. It sure wasn't Dublin, where everyone looked and sounded the same.[4]

Cecelia liked the hubbub, since so much of it seemed to come from children—hundreds of them! When she went to work at Fort Snelling she imagined she would be the only girl there. In fact, quite a number of children lived in the garrison. There was Rose Angelica Gear, whose father—the fort's chaplain, Rev. Ezekiel Gear—was so grand and imposing. Henry Eskeltson, an Irish boy of 12, lived with his mother and his soldier father, but Cecelia hardly ever saw him. Everyone said that he'd gone wild, like a lot of other boys. Ann McGee, another daughter of Erin, was just about Cecelia's age. Her father was a soldier, too, but unlike most of the others had a sizable family living with him. A soldier's meager pay meant that hiring help was out of the question, so Ann—the oldest of four—became the family's servant girl. Cecelia could count none of these children as friends. Friends were for girls who had time. She was no longer a child, and she sure didn't have any time.[5]

Cecelia snapped out of her daydreaming when Mrs. Kirkham called her upstairs to meet a visitor. Now this was unusual, Cecelia thought. Not even those nosy Kirkham relatives who had come out recently from Boston on a tour of the river valley had wanted to meet the hired help.

Sitting stiffly in the parlor with both the captain and Mrs. Kirkham was a neatly dressed man who was introduced as Mr. Henry L. Tilden. He was talking about how tired he was, having spent most of that day and the one before at the garrison enumerating for the U.S. census, counting all of the people in the year-old Minnesota Territory. Cecelia was surprised to hear some of the questions he was asking the captain, such as how much his property was worth. She was even more surprised to hear the captain, after shifting in his chair and clearing his throat, reply that he thought it to be about a thousand dollars. A thousand dollars! Cecelia couldn't even count that high and was sure she would never see that kind of money in her lifetime.[6]

Daydreaming again. The autumn light was fading. Mrs. Kirkham motioned to Cecelia to light the lamp on the table so Mr. Tilden could see as he carefully copied the Kirkhams' answers into his ledger-like book.

Brass thimble and plated-brass pins with hand-wound heads from early Fort Snelling

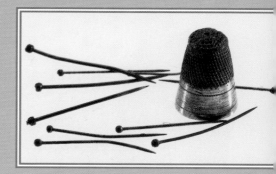

Engraving of Fort Snelling from *Harper's New Monthly Magazine*, July 1853. The officers' quarters are immediately to the right of the commandant's house at rear, center.

Mrs. Kirkham answered for Cecelia, but on her last word she was interrupted by a snort from Mr. Tilden. "Irish?" he repeated. He could hardly disguise his disgust. "Why, that's—what? Let me see. . . Yes, the eleventh one today. What a way to end the day!" The Kirkhams looked uncomfortable but made no move to stop his tirade, issued freely, as if Cecelia had disappeared into the stone walls. Mr. Tilden said that cities back East were flooding with dim-witted, ape-like, drunken, lazy, starving Irish. He told a joke he had heard in a minstrel show about a Negro complaining that his master was treating him as badly as if he were a common Irishman. Capt. Kirkham, in answer, could only say that he hoped Mr. Tilden would be able to sleep off some of his disgust with Paddies, since nearly half of the people he would be counting tomorrow in the rest of the garrison were Irish. The captain considered warning Tilden that he would also be meeting a couple of Irish convicts in the guardhouse, but then thought better of it.[7]

After Mr. Tilden left with the captain, Mrs. Kirkham tried to smooth over the enumerator's rough words, telling Cecelia that he hadn't meant anything by it, but Cecelia's mind was already somewhere else. She thought about her father, who had so fiercely held to a vision of Americans as heroes, a picture that today, in this place, had become a little more tarnished. 🦋

—*Brian Horrigan*

NOTES

[1] Patricia C. Harpole and Mary D. Nagle, eds., *Minnesota Territorial Census, 1850* (St. Paul: Minnesota Historical Society, 1972), 14, lists 13-year-old Cecelia O'Brien, born in Ireland, as a member of the Fort Snelling household of Capt. Kirkham, along with his wife, daughter, and 20-year-old Fanny Bisoiner. A 40-year-old Irish woman named Catharine O'Brien is listed in the Sibley household in Mendota (p. 11). This fictional account uses the actual names and ages of Fort Snelling residents and the census enumerator.

[2] The quote about soldiering is from Thomas D'Arcy McGee, *A History of the Irish Settlers in North America from the Earliest Period to the Census of 1850* (Boston: Patrick Donohoe, 1852), 191. U.S. Army Capt. John Paul Jones O'Brien, born in Philadelphia of Irish parents, was decorated for his role in the Battle of Buena Vista in 1847; F. B. Heitman, *Historical Register of the United States Army* (Washington, D.C.: National Tribune, 1890), 497.

[3] Thomas Hamilton, a British traveler in the U.S., wrote in 1834: "Domestic service . . . is considered degrading by all [Americans] untainted with the curse of African descent"; quoted in David R. Roediger, *The Wages of Whiteness: Race and the Making of the American Working Class* (New York: Verso, 1991), 145–46. For more on Irish immigrants and domestic service, see *Wages of Whiteness*, 133–63; Hasia R. Diner, *Erin's Daughters in America: Irish Immigrant Women in the Nineteenth Century* (Baltimore: Johns Hopkins University Press, 1983), 80–94. For a full-scale fictional treatment of an Irish servant's life in the 1850s, see Mary Anne Sadlier's *Bessy Conway; Or, the Irish Girl in America* (1861). The complete text, along with commentaries on Sadlier's work and historical context, can be found online at http://xroads.virginia.edu/~HYPER/hypertex.html.

[4] On the steamboat and the buildings, see J. Fletcher Williams, *A History of the City of Saint Paul to 1875* (1876; reprint, St. Paul: Minnesota Historical Society Press, 1983), 259, 224.

[5] For the names and ages of children at Fort Snelling, see Harpole and Nagle, eds., *Minnesota Territorial Census*, 14–15. On wild boys, see E. Anthony Rotundo, *American Manhood: Transformations in Masculinity from the Revolution to the Modern Era* (New York: Basic Books, 1993), 31–55; Col. John H. Bliss, "Reminiscences of Fort Snelling," in *Minnesota Historical Society Collections* 6 (St. Paul, 1894): 335–53.

[6] Henry L. Tilden enumerated Dahkotah County, which included Fort Snelling and vicinity; Harpole and Nagle, eds., *Minnesota Territorial Census*, viii. The census also recorded the value of a person's real estate in dollars. On Kirkham's property, presumably in his native Massachusetts, see *Minnesota Territorial Census*, 14.

[7] On anti-Irish attitudes at midcentury, see Roediger, *Wages of Whiteness*, 133–56. The minstrel-show joke is quoted in Noel Ignatiev, *How the Irish Became White* (New York: Routledge, 1995), 42. For the Irish soldiers at Fort Snelling, see Harpole and Nagle, eds., *Minnesota Territorial Census*, 14–17.

A DAY IN THE LIFE *of*

Helen Nelson

HELENA CHRISTINA NILSSON, now Helen Nelson, sat on a bench in the afternoon shade on September 17, 1852, smelling the fragrance of the sun-warmed pine logs in her family's new house at Hay Lake. Blackbirds chattered across the harvested field, eating scattered bits of grain. They were probably getting ready to go south for the winter, as far as Moline where she and her family had lived, or even farther south to St. Louis or New Orleans, where her fiancé Frederick had traveled after he left Germany.[1]

Beyond the field and the birds she could see clusters of yellow flowers and beyond them, by Hay Lake, clumps of blue. Miss Stevenson, the niece of Taylors Falls businessman W. H. C. Folsom, had told her the names of the flowers—the yellow ones were sunflowers and goldenrod, the blue ones, fringed gentians, and the plants with the little whisks of white feathers scattering in the breeze were milkweeds. The colors were those of the comforter she had finished making only last week.[2]

Miss Stevenson had showed her the sticky "milk" in the milkweed, and it reminded her of their cow, happily wandering around in her wood-fenced enclosure near the barn. How good it was to have their own milk, and how clever her father had been to buy the cow at Moline and bring her all the way to Minnesota on the steamboat. Her father had split fifteen hundred fence rails to pay for that cow. Today her younger sister would do the milking. Her mother and sisters could do the housework, the cooking and cleaning, and everything else that needed to be done for

Helen Nelson Lammers,
later in life

tomorrow. She, Helen Nelson, was finished working for other people, even her family. Beginning tomorrow she would be Mrs. Frederick Lammers and would work only for herself and her husband.[3]

She could hear her father beyond the barn, cutting logs on the edge of their pine woods and talking to Oscar Roos. When her family had come to Minnesota not much more than a year ago, her father had earned enough money carpentering in Marine Mills to pay for their land. He and a hired man had cut down the trees and built their new house and barn. Now he was starting another building, maybe a workshop with a room for Oscar when he came to see them. Oscar was the last of the Swede

boys who had made them welcome when they arrived in Hay Lake last spring. None of the three young men were any good as farmers, and they had been glad to sell their land and little log house to her family. Carl Fernstrom and August Sandahl had gone south, but Oscar liked to be with her family and stayed in Minnesota. He called her mother, Margreta, "Mor Greta," and she treated him like a son. Frederick liked Oscar, too, and was going to help him find work in the woods. Oscar was nice enough but not at all interesting compared to Frederick.[4]

Helen let herself remember when Oscar was in Taylors Falls and she met Frederick with him at Mr. Folsom's store. It was soon after she went to work for the Folsoms and was living in the family's maid's room upstairs over the store. The Pioneer Store building was next to the St. Croix River, and from her window she could see the landing where the steamboats docked and the logs came tumbling down from the logging camps as soon as the ice was gone in the spring.[5]

There was always excitement in and around Mr. Folsom's store. Everyone shopped there and found almost anything one would want. And everyone called for mail at the little post office in a corner of the store. Oscar got a letter from Sweden, and Frederick had one from Germany the day she first met him. She had finished her housework for Mrs. Folsom and gone downstairs to wander through the store, trying to decide what she would buy with her pay. After their first meeting,

Frederick stopped to see her whenever he came into town from his logging camp. At first they didn't talk much. Her English wasn't very good—she only knew what she needed to understand Mrs. Folsom—but Frederick had been in America for 10 years and his English was excellent. Oscar's was good, too, and he translated for them. Soon Frederick picked up more Swedish and they didn't have any trouble talking together. He didn't say much about himself, but Oscar told her he had been well educated in Germany and had even studied Greek and Latin. Mrs. Folsom said he came from a good family and his name was really Von Lammers, whatever that meant.[6]

Whenever she had a day off work, Oscar and Frederick drove her to Hay Lake to see her family. Another time Frederick went hunting and brought her family some venison and pigeons. The Nelsons all seemed to like him. By midsummer she and Frederick had decided to be married, but she planned to stay on with the Folsoms until she had the clothes she wanted. She bought a beautiful woolen shawl with her first month's wages. Another month she got wristlets, gloves, shoes, a pretty brooch, a back comb, and some whalebones to wear for a more fashionable figure. Then she chose calico, buttons, and ribbons for one dress and gingham for an everyday housedress, the one she was wearing this September day. Later, when she began to plan for her marriage, she chose nicer materials, and her mother's friend, who was a very good dressmaker, told her what she should buy for her wedding dress.[7]

After Frederick took her out to see the house near the Marine Mills road where he and Mr. Porter, his American partner, were living when they came in from the logging camp, she couldn't imagine how the two men could keep house with so little of what she considered necessary. She began to buy what she would need for housekeeping: sheets, towels, flat irons, a laundry tub and washboard, a tea canister, plates, cups, spoons, preserve dishes, yard goods for curtains, a comforter. She and Frederick chose six straight chairs, a rocking chair, and a big mirror; she also selected a poker, shovel, and tongs for their new stove. Mr. Folsom's clerk noted in his journal that Frederick would pay for the goods but delivery would be made to Helen Nelson.[8]

The house would be a satisfactory home, although she and Frederick agreed that it needed to be cleaned and repaired. Frederick promised that Mr. Porter would soon move out so that they could do the work. Finally, she was pleased to see him at Folsom's store buying a trunk and carpetbag.[9] Soon after he moved out of the house, and she and Frederick had time to clean and paint, repair the broken windows, and arrange the furniture. Her mother and sisters helped make the window curtains and put the new dishes in the cupboard. Frederick bought new locks for the doors.

When her friends at Moline heard about her wedding plans, they wrote: "From all we can learn of Mr. Lammers we feel assured that you will have a good husband." She could have answered their letter in English, but it was really too much work. There would be plenty of time to learn English after she was married.

Calico dress from the 1860s

Page from the Folsom store's ledger book detailing some of Helen Nelson's purchases, 1852

Frederick had ordered two McGuffey readers to teach her, but since he understood so much Swedish now, why bother? Her friends in Moline understood. They hoped she would continue her studies, but if she had no time, they wrote, "We shall be much obliged to your new husband to do it for you." Frederick wrote easily and seemed to enjoy doing it. After all the cleaning and washing and cooking she had done for Mrs. Folsom and the cleaning and painting and sewing for their house, she didn't feel at all guilty about sitting in the shade doing nothing and thinking only in Swedish.[10]

She had left the Folsoms at the end of August, only a few weeks ago. On August 28, she persuaded Frederick to buy some new clothes for himself. The clothes he wore every day were right for the lumber camp and the woods—and even for daily life in Taylors Falls—but he certainly could afford something better for his wedding. Their Swedish neighbors would be much impressed. She helped him choose a new wardrobe: a dress coat and pants, a silk vest, a silk cravat and handkerchief, a hat, socks, a white shirt, and a new carpetbag for traveling.[11]

At first they talked of going to Stillwater or St. Paul to be married and then taking a wedding trip somewhere by steamboat. Her parents did not like that plan; they wanted her to be married at home at a time when Pastor Gustaf Unonius would be visiting the Swedes at Chisago Lakes. He could as well come to Hay Lake and stay at their house, so she and Frederick needn't go running off to the city to find a pastor. Frederick was willing. She would have liked having the wedding day only for themselves, but the neighbors insisted that the pastor should christen their children at the same time. He would be the first pastor they had seen since they left Moline. Her mother liked the new plan because the families of the children would bring food for the celebration. So the wedding and christenings were set for the day after Pastor Unonius visited Chisago Lakes.[12]

One other decision needed to be made: where to go for the wedding trip. Helen wasn't excited about going anywhere. She and her family had done a lot of traveling in the last two years since sailing from Sweden on the *Sofie*.[13] They had traveled across half of America to Moline and then come up the Mississippi and St. Croix Rivers to Marine Mills. Why not travel to Taylors Falls, to their own house, all freshly cleaned and painted with new curtains on new windows? Frederick was agreeable. It was good to have all the decisions made.

She could hear her mother and her elder sister bustling around in the house getting supper. Her younger sister had come out with a pail on the way to milk the cow. Her father had stopped his work. He and Oscar had washed and combed their hair at the basin by the back door and were coming to sit by her on the bench, waiting for the guests. Any time now a neighbor would drive in from Chisago Lakes bringing Pastor Unonius, and Frederick would be coming down the Marine road from Taylors Falls. There were no clouds in the sky. September 18 would be a sunny wedding day for Frederick Lammers and Helen Nelson, the first Swedish bride in territorial Minnesota.[14]

—*Helen McCann White*

NOTES

[1] Daniel Nilsson and his family emigrated from Norrbo in Helsingland, Sweden, in 1850, settling first in Moline, Illinois; Conrad Bergendoff, trans., *The Pioneer Swedish Settlements and Swedish Lutheran Churches in America, 1845–1860*, selected chapters of vol. 1 of Eric Norelius, *De Svenska Luterska Församlingarnas och Svenskarnes Historia I Amerika* (1890) (Rock Island, Ill.: Augustana Historical Society, 1984), 295. Frederick Lammers emigrated to America in 1843, stopping first at New Orleans and then St. Louis; Louis F. Lammers, "Lammers Family History" (1910), with later research notes by Stanley Selin, a Nelson relative, copies in Selin's possession.

[2] A transaction between Harriet Stevenson and Helen Nelson is recorded in ledger, vol. 23, Aug. 20, 1852, W. H. C. Folsom and Family Papers, Minnesota Historical Society (MHS); W. H. C. Folsom, *Fifty Years in the Northwest* (St. Paul: Pioneer Press Co., 1888), 341–42.

[3] Bergendoff, *Pioneer Swedish Settlements*, 295.

[4] On Roos, Fernstrom, and Sandahl, see "Swedish Pioneer Remembered," *Dalles Visitor* (Taylors Falls), 1975, p. 16; John Larson, "Oscar Roos' Origins: Conflicting Tales," based on additional research in Sweden, corrects errors in the *Dalles Visitor* story, manuscript in Larson's possession; Charles Fernstrom to Oscar Roos, Sept. 11, 1892, and Roos to Frederick Lammers, Nov. 22, Dec. 4, 1892, copies in Selin's possession.

[5] Folsom built the first frame building in Taylors Falls as a combined residence and store and opened for business in Sept. 1850; he and his family later moved to a new home, today an MHS historic site, in what is now the Angel Hill Historic District.

[6] Lammers, "Lammers Family History." The Taylors Falls Post Office opened in the Folsom store in Mar. 1851; Folsom, *Fifty Years,* 332.

[7] Helen Nelson's "settlement" is entered on Aug. 14, 1852, W. H. C. Folsom blotters, vols. 3 and 4, Taylors Falls Historical Society (TFHS). This is a different group of volumes from the series at MHS.

[8] Beginning in May 1849, Lammers traded at the Dexter and Harrington general store in St. Croix Falls; journal, p. 64 and following, Dexter, Harrington and Co. Papers, MHS. On Aug. 18, 1851, he and his partner James Porter purchased outfitting supplies from Folsom; ledger, vol. 37, TFHS. Numerous household items purchased on Aug. 14, 1852, were charged to Lammers and Porter but marked "Delivered to Helen Nelson"; see also Aug. 28, 1852—both ledger, vol. 23, Folsom papers, MHS.

[9] Porter bought a trunk on Sept. 11, 1852; Folsom blotter, vol. 5, TFHS.

[10] E. K. Babbitt to Helen Lammers, Jan. 26, 1853, copy in Selin's possession. Lammers was charged for two McGuffey readers and a geography and a spelling book on Oct. 12, 1852; Folsom blotter, vol. 5, TFHS. In the Lammers family papers, Selin has found no letters written in English by Helen Nelson Lammers; Selin to the author, Dec. 20, 1997.

[11] Ledger, vol. 23, Aug. 18, 1852, Folsom papers, MHS.

[12] The Rev. Gustaf Unonius, then an Episcopalian minister in Chicago, encouraged early immigrant Swedes to move to Minnesota; for his visit to the Chisago Lakes settlement and Hay Lake, see Bergendoff, *Pioneer Swedish Settlements*, 261–62; *"The Heritage of a Century": The History of the Elim Lutheran Church, Scandia, Minnesota* (1954), n.p.

[13] Bergendoff, *Pioneer Swedish Settlements*, 295.

[14] For more on the Lammers couple, see Helen M. White, "The Occurrence on Lammers Farm," *Dalles Visitor* 30 (Summer 1998): 9–10.

Minnesota's Territ

"**T**hirty Hours From St. Paul to Chicago! Snake Ejected From a Man's Stomach. New Liquor Law in Maine. More Indians Killed. Grand Celebration: Mississippi River Wire Suspension Bridge. The Secret of Matrimonial Happiness. A Simple Yet Certain Cure For Piles. To Make Tomato Figs. Civil War in Kansas/Lawrence Destroyed: Free State Blood Spilt. A Nobleman of Sense. Look at This! No Murder!" These news and advertising headlines from the columns of Minnesota's earliest newspapers illustrate frontier journalism's curious and diffuse

JANE LAMM CARROLL

orial Newspapers

content. The territorial press conveyed
information, provided entertainment,
offered advice to lovers and prescriptions
for the good life, titillated with stories of
the sensational and macabre, advertised
local businesses and the latest patent
medicines, sung Minnesota's praises to
encourage immigration, and voiced fiercely partisan views on local and national
political issues.

Territorial printing tools: hand press made by Cincinnati
Typefoundry about 1836, reputed to be the one James M.
Goodhue used to print the *Minnesota Pioneer*; and Goodhue's
type arrayed on an early issue of his newspaper.

Like other midnineteenth-century American newspapers, Minnesota's territorial papers differed from modern ones in important ways. First, there was little attempt at "objective" reporting; readers expected and got news conveyed with a heavy dose of editorial comment. Second, papers were ferociously partisan, routinely attacking political opponents in a manner that readers today might find shocking and inappropriately personal. Finally, "news" 150 years ago was often based on nothing more than conjecture or hearsay; much of it would not meet current journalism standards.

While today the most significant news appears on the paper's first page, that is not the way Minnesota's early editors organized their publications. Indeed, they gave a relatively meager amount of space to the news, often burying the most important stories on the second page amidst advertising, legal notices, sentimental fiction, recipes, and trivial items. But in the 1850s Minnesota newspapers were not primarily interested in reporting news. Rather, they aimed to promote the territory and act as a partisan voice in an era when newspapers were the only mass medium through which political parties could influence people.[1]

Between 1849, when James. M Goodhue started the *Minnesota Pioneer,* the territory's first newspaper, and 1857, the last full year of the territory, settlers established 82 newspapers in Minnesota. Of these, about 70 were published weekly, six daily, and the rest biweekly, triweekly, monthly, or irregularly. Unlike today's corporate-owned conglomerates, these were generally independent enterprises, owned and operated by one or two persons.[2]

At first, all of Minnesota's newspapers were weeklies; many later developed into dailies as the population expanded. St. Paul was home to 21 papers during the territorial period, including the German publications *Minnesota Deutsche Zeitung* and *Minnesota National Demokrat,* and the Norwegian *Folkets Röst.* The capital saw four daily publications established in 1854 alone. St. Anthony produced four newspapers and Minneapolis, two. Newspapers did not appear outside of these three locations until 1854, then multiplied rapidly as the territory's population increased dramatically and settlement spread up and down Minnesota's rivers. Between 1854 and 1860, almost 100 English and several foreign-language weeklies were established. Red Wing had five newspapers, including the Swedish-language *Minnesota Posten.* Stillwater, Winona, Shakopee, and Carimona (Fillmore County) each had three, and Rochester, St. Peter, Faribault, Hastings, St. Cloud, Monticello, Cannon Falls, Read's Landing/Wabasha, and Chatfield had two apiece. Towns with one newspaper included Sauk Rapids, Brownsville, Nininger, Lake City, Albert Lea, Preston, Traverse des Sioux, Wasioja, Oronoco, Owatonna, Bancroft, Belle Plaine, Glencoe, Hokah, Henderson, Watab/Little Falls, Mankato, and Mantorville. Chaska produced a German-language newspaper, the *Minnesota Thalboten.* This proliferation indicates a relatively high literacy rate among settlers. As John P. Owens, editor of the *Weekly Minnesotian* (St. Paul), observed, "The people of Minnesota are remarkable for the liberality with which they support their local newspapers."

Minnesota's first German-language newspaper, begun in St. Paul in 1855

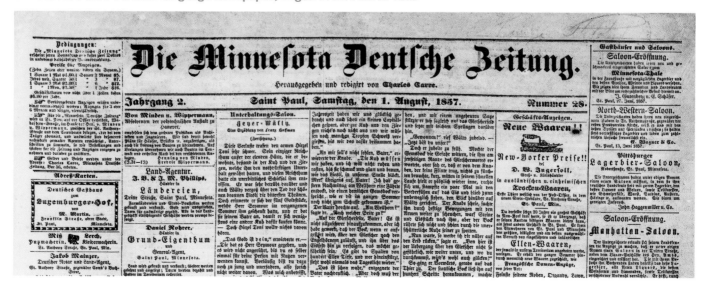

St. Cloud Democrat office and home of its founder, the fiery Jane Grey Swisshelm, about 1858. An abolitionist and suffragist, Swisshelm was the territory's first newspaperwoman.

Local as these papers were, they relied heavily on national and international news, as well as other items clipped from eastern and downriver publications. Indeed, these clippings provided the bulk of the frontier newspaper's contents. Until linked to the telegraph in 1860, Minnesota editors relied on the mail to bring them other papers. This meant that there was a lag in the news of a few days during the navigation season and a week, at minimum, during winter. Mail traveled to the farthest point west via railroad, thence overland and upriver to Minnesota. The first railroad to reach the Mississippi River arrived at Rock Island, Illinois, in 1854. By 1857 the railroad had reached Prairie du Chien, Wisconsin, but the mail still had to travel more than 200 miles by steamboat up the Mississippi or overland via sleigh. Dubuque, Iowa, and LaCrosse, Wisconsin, were the closest telegraph termini in the 1850s, and the *Dubuque Daily Express and Herald* was the closest "big city" newspaper.[3]

Early editors depended on outside sources for more than their news. Printing presses, type, paper, and ink all came from distant cities such as Cincinnati and Boston. The equipment could be transported only during navigation season, due to the high cost of shipping overland in the winter. No local newsprint was available locally until 1859, when a paper mill on Hennepin Island began production. Sometimes editors had to make their own ink until a new supply could be obtained.[4]

Although markedly partisan in tone, Minnesota's territorial newspapers were otherwise very similar. They were generally two or four pages long; page dimensions of weeklies measured 20-by-25 inches, and dailies were generally 15-by-21—both larger than today's standard newspaper. Each page held six or seven columns broken sporadically into separate items usually identified by a brief title. Rarely was there enough on any one subject to fill an entire column, advertisements excepted. No large headlines adorned the front page as in today's papers. Instead, first pages were devoted to clipped national and international news stories, as well as fiction and poetry. The second page contained national and local news, editorials, advertisements, legal notices, recipes, more fiction and poetry, proscriptive literature, and sensational items. Third and fourth pages generally consisted entirely of advertisements.[5]

THROUGHOUT THE TERRITORIAL ERA, editors promoted Minnesota as a desirable place to settle, filling their columns with detailed descriptions of the

The outspoken
James M. Goodhue, about 1850

region's natural beauty, abundant resources, fertile soil, and healthy climate. Goodhue of the *Minnesota Pioneer* was the most frequent and enthusiastic booster. He explored the region by horseback, steamboat, and canoe, returning to St. Paul to report to the world what he had seen. Ever aware of an eastern audience that included potential immigrants, Goodhue tended to embellish his descriptions. In August 1849 he ended a long and comprehensive recital of Minnesota's virtues by extolling its climate and many waterways:

Farmers, especially of New England, if they could but once see our lands, would never think of settling on the bilious bottoms and the enervating prairies south of us. What is fertility, what is wealth, without vigorous health and activity of body and mind? These are considerations that will weigh more in the future with the immigrants, than they hitherto have: a clear, bracing air, an invigorating winter to give elasticity to the system—and water as pure and soft as the dews of heaven, gushing from hill and valley.[6]

Editorial opinion did not stop with boosterism. Any and all news was subject to comment. Reporting on a ball held at St. Paul's Central House, Goodhue opined: "Dancing, properly conducted, with chaste, correct music, has a tendency, not only to improve the manners, but to elevate, to etherialize the mind."[7] Reports on the weather, conditions about town, and local events also reflected the editor's personality. Earle S. Goodrich, editor of St. Paul's *Daily Pioneer and Democrat,* offered the following observations on life in St. Paul on May 30, 1857: "Third Street was kept yesterday in passable and comfortable condition, by the sprinkling wagon, thanks to somebody," and "The sun shone out brightly and warm, but the gentle wind abstracted the caloric, and made street walking pleasant."

Minnesotian editor Owens declared his indignation after reporting the death of a man stabbed in a saloon brawl: "If no man present at the drunken row on Tuesday night had carried about his person a concealed and deadly weapon, in all human probability no one would

Minnesota Pioneer, September 6, 1849, with columns of small, dense type typical of the era's newspapers

Earle S. Goodrich, the *Minnesota Pioneer*'s third editor who introduced a daily edition and merged the paper with the rival *Minnesota Democrat* in 1855. The newspaper shop was located at Third and Jackson Streets, St. Paul.

have been killed. What a solemn protest is here against this horrible practice! What need has any man with a knife or pistol in St. Paul?" M. H. Abbott, the *St. Croix Union*'s editor, lectured the men of Stillwater on relations between the sexes: "A lady's heart is a delicate institution and should be treated as such. There are some brutal specimens of corduroy that seem to think the little beater made to toss around like a joke, a glove or a bootjack. Young man, if you don't intend to take it to the milliner and parson, just let Miss What's-her-name's heart alone— right off too."[8]

THE OPENLY PARTISAN nineteenth-century newspapers often adopted their party's name as their title. But whether or not the title identified the newspaper as Democrat, Whig, or Republican, it would not have taken a reader long to ascertain a paper's affiliation. Editors did not hesitate to attack political enemies, including rival newspapermen, in robust, if not rancorous, terms. Daniel A.

Robertson of St. Paul's *Minnesota Democrat* had the following to say about Goodhue in 1851: "His inveterate propensity to gratify petty malignity, and personal hate, in the columns of his paper, renders him incapable of conducting a decent and honorable press." In 1851 Goodhue himself was stabbed and nearly killed as the result of his verbal attacks on Judge David Cooper, which included the following assessment of the judge's character:

> He is not only a miserable drunkard, who habitually gets so drunk as to *feel upward* for the ground, but he also spends days and nights and Sunday, playing cards in groceries [saloons]. He is lost to all sense of decency and respect. *Off* the Bench he is a beast, and *on* the Bench he is an ass, stuffed with arrogance, self conceit and a ridiculous affectation of dignity.[9]

Before 1855 Democrats wielded most of the power in Minnesota. The founding of the territory coincided with the waning years of the Whig Party, which was increasingly split between North and South over slavery. Consequently, although there were prominent Whigs in Minnesota, including the territory's first governor, Alexander Ramsey, factions within the Democratic Party, led by Henry H. Sibley and Henry M. Rice, dominated politics. These factions were known as the "Fur" (Sibley) and "Anti-Fur" (Rice) parties because they grew out of a long-standing rivalry between the two men that had its roots in their involvement in the fur trade.[10]

These contingents were occasionally challenged by other Democrats and on particular issues would ally themselves with the minority Whigs. Although Goodhue had previously published a Whig paper in Lancaster,

Minneapolis's *Minnesota Democrat,* at Second and Washington Avenues looking east to the more populous St. Anthony, 1857. Established in 1856, the newspaper was an ancestor of the current *Star Tribune.*

Wisconsin, he discovered upon his arrival in Minnesota that the real power lay with the Democrats and quickly aligned himself with Sibley. In 1849 the first St. Paul newspaper to provide a political alternative to Goodhue's *Pioneer* was the *Chronicle* (later the *Chronicle and Register*), edited by John P. Owens, a staunch Whig. Although Owens's first newspaper lasted only two years, in 1851 he became editor of the *Minnesotian,* which would become one of the territory's most prominent publications. Robertson, who had founded the *Minnesota Democrat* in 1850, quickly became Goodhue's chief rival within that party.[11]

In the first years of the territory, Minnesota editors were very parochial in their partisanship; curiously, they had little to say about slavery at a time when that issue was tearing the nation apart and dominating national politics. Instead, they sparred over local matters, including allegations of corruption by officials, efforts to remove Chief Justice Aaron Goodrich from the territorial supreme court, and charges of fraud in the 1851 Indian treaties. Minnesota's politicians and editors were reluctant to speak out about slavery, fearing that they might offend congressmen and harm the territory's interests (especially appropriations). But this reticence ended in 1854 as the nation erupted in response to the passage of the Kansas-Nebraska Act.[12]

Senator Stephen A. Douglas's measure repealed the 1820 Missouri Compromise line, which had prohibited the introduction of slavery above 36°30′ north latitude in the Louisiana Purchase lands (excepting Missouri) and introduced popular sovereignty as the means for deciding whether slavery would be allowed in new states. Thus, the Kansas and Nebraska Territories could now be organized as slave states if settlers so chose. Pro- and antislavery settlers streamed into Kansas and began killing each other, and "Bleeding Kansas" became the focus of the nation. Unable to respond to the crisis, the Whig Party finally collapsed. In the North a new party, the Republicans, formed around the primary aim of stopping the extension of slavery into the nation's territories. In July 1855 Minnesota Republicans held their first convention, adopting a platform that denounced the repeal of the Missouri Compromise and the extension of slavery and demanded repeal of the 1850 Fugitive Slave law.[13]

John P. Owens, about 1880

Minnesota editors jumped into the political fray. St. Paul's *Daily Pioneer* and, later, the *Daily Pioneer and Democrat* claimed to oppose the extension of slavery but at the same time vehemently attacked abolitionism. Most of Minnesota's Democratic papers took the position that the Constitution protected slavery where it already existed, and most supported popular sovereignty. The *Minnesotian* and the *St. Paul Daily Times* sympathized with abolitionism and generally supported the Republican view. In May 1855 the *Times* encouraged Minnesotans to go to Kansas and fight proslavery forces. A few months later it cried: "Let the Slave Oligarchy continue its course in Kansas, and if the Federal Government does not interfere, civil war will follow. The whole power of the North will be brought to bear against this den of iniquity." When the national Democratic Party split over President James Buchanan's support of the fraudulent proslavery LeCompton Constitution for Kansas, the *Pioneer and Democrat* firmly backed Douglas's contention that the constitution violated the principle of popular sovereignty.[14]

Partisanship on the slavery issue continued in Minnesota newspapers as the territory prepared for statehood. In the summer of 1857, Minnesota Republicans and Democrats held rival constitutional conventions, each party hoping that the new state would enter the Union under its auspices. Coverage of the two conventions followed partisan lines, with some newspapers failing to report at all on the proceedings of the opposing convention. In his July 17 edition, Earle Goodrich justified the *Daily Pioneer and Democrat*'s omission of news on the Republican convention: "We find on perusing the report of the Republican gathering, prepared for our paper, so many glaring and mendacious misrepresentations, that we do not think our duty as journalist would justify in giving further currency to their slanderous lies."[15]

Throughout the debate over the state constitution, Minnesota Democrats and Republicans reviled one another in the press. The *Pioneer and Democrat* frequently raised the race issue, calling its opponents "Black Republicans," who would allow "niggers" to vote and framing the issue as "White Supremacy against Negro Equality." In fact, the Republicans themselves split over black suffrage, resulting in a constitutional compromise

Around the territory and into statehood, newspapers boldly proclaimed their party affiliation.

that retained the word "white" as a qualification for voting but allowed for later consideration of the issue in a referendum. For their part, Republican editors referred to the Democrats as "dough faces" (a term commonly used to refer to Northerners sympathetic to slave owners) and "bootlicks."[16]

In the last years before statehood there was also vigorous debate in Minnesota newspapers over the proposed boundaries of the new state and an attempt to move the capital from St. Paul to St. Peter. Settlers in southern Minnesota favored an east-west line at about the 46th parallel, while others advocated a north-south line running along the Red River Valley south to Iowa. An east-west boundary would have placed St. Peter near the center of the new state while marginalizing St. Paul. Faced with this threat, the bitterly partisan St. Paul newspapers closed ranks against southern Minnesotans. The editor of the *Winona Argus* expressed his disgust with St. Paul's champions, describing them as "a corrupt gang of political knaves who have congregated about the gotham of Minnesota." Especially at fault, according to the *Argus,* was Henry M. Rice, Minnesota's delegate to Congress:

> We have long felt convinced that Southern Minnesota occupied but a small share of Mr. Rice's thoughts, except such as were devoted to the contrivance of schemes and plots counter to her interests . . . but we must confess that this secretly concocted and treacherous movement [to keep the capital in St. Paul] this stealthy, midnight, and assassin-like charge upon a confiding and unguarded constituency, in the shape of an attempt to render us yet more dependent upon a set of political schemers and tricksters whose presumption, venality and corruption hath had no equal since the cackling of the geese at Rome.[17]

In fact, the boundary dispute divided northern and southern Minnesotans of both parties. In July, for example, the Republican *St. Peter Free Press* warned Republicans that, if they approved a north-south boundary, southern Minnesotans would "fight it to the death." Yet the controversy also had partisan implications; a north-south line ensured the dominance of the Democrats, whose strength was in St. Paul and to the north, while southern Minnesota was heavily Republican. In the end, both conventions adopted the north-south boundary, after which not much was said on the subject.[18]

PERUSING THE COLUMNS of Minnesota's early newspapers provides a fascinating glimpse into everyday life in the 1850s. The diversity of Minnesota's territorial population is evident. In 1849, for example, when the French-Canadian and Indian populations were still large and influential, the *Minnesota Chronicle and Register* of St. Paul reported on the opening of district court at Mendota: "A number of jurors not understanding the English language, W. H. Forbes, Esq., acted as interpreter. He explained to the jury in a very satisfactory manner we are told, in the French language, the nature and impact of the oath they were about to take."[19]

Newspapers frequently reported on fighting between the Ojibwe and Dakota and on other activities of these tribes and the Winnebago (Ho-Chunk). Most stories about Indians were bigoted; even attempts at praise were tinged with racism. In 1851, for instance, the *Minnesota Democrat* reported:

> Batiste, the celebrated Winnebago chief, was in town last week. He is a noble looking son of the forest. He speaks several Indian languages, also the French, and understands English tolerably. His father was a Frenchman, and his mother a full blood Winnebago. He is 37 years of age, very intelligent for an Indian, and a great favorite among the whites. He lives with his band numbering 114 at Long Prairie.[20]

City and town ordinances, published in their entirety in the newspapers, reveal something of the health and safety conditions in Minnesota's frontier communities. In 1855, for example, Stillwater prohibited hogs from running in the streets and provided the marshal a $1 fee for each animal he impounded. The city also forbade blasting or quarrying rock within its limits "so as in any manner to endanger the life or limbs of any person passing along such street, alley, or highway," as well as rolling rocks or stones down the sides of a bluff onto any thoroughfare. Among many other ordinances, St. Anthony outlawed the deposit of any "dung, dead animal, carion [*sic*], putrid meat or fish, entrails or decayed vegetables" in its avenues. Racing carriages and driving faster than six miles per hour were also prohibited. The *Minnesotian* reported an improvement for St. Paul pedestrians in 1853, through the efforts of two "gallant and commendable gentlemen":

> There has heretofore been, in muddy times, an "impassable gulf," for ladies at least, between the upper and lower extremes of town. . . . This inconvenience is to be done away with . . . with a plank walk, which will make the promenade complete and continuous from the corner of Third and Robert streets to the top of the hill at Maj. Fridley's dwelling.[21]

TERRITORIAL NEWSPAPER READERS were treated to a fair share of the sensational and macabre. The number of

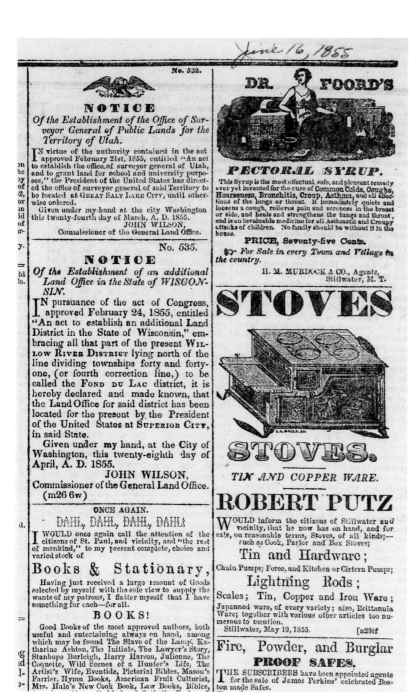

Miscellaneous advertisements and notices from Stillwater's weekly *St. Croix Union*, June 16, 1855, page 3

such stories varied greatly from issue to issue, depending upon how much space an editor had to fill with clippings from eastern newspapers. Bloody murders, murder trials, massacres, seductions, divorce and adultery cases, and news of the weird were standard fare.

Typically brief, these stories usually had catchy headlines. The *St. Anthony Express*, for example, reproduced a story from an eastern newspaper, headlined, "A SNAKE EJECTED FROM A MAN'S STOMACH": "A Mr. Wade, in Virginia, has, by the aid of a vomiting emetic, succeeded in vomiting a load from his stomach, which proves to be a snake."[22]

Advertising was more genteel and understated than today; many territorial-era ads now read more like formal invitations or thank-you notes:

> The Proprietors of this truly Minnesota River Boat, take this opportunity for tendering their sincere thanks for the very liberal patronage they received during the last season, and now have the pleasure of announcing to the shippers of St. Paul and the inhabitants of the Minnesota Valley, that they are refitting and refurnishing the Steamer Equator in a superior manner, and will be in readiness upon the opening of navigation, to resume her regular trips on the Minnesota River.[23]

Advertisements for retail businesses were similarly refined, especially when addressing female customers: "TO THE LADIES: Mrs. M. L. Stoakes wishes to inform her friends and patrons that she has just returned from New York, with a large stock of the Most Fashionable Millinery Goods that could be found in that city. Ladies, please call and see for yourselves on Friday, May 22d."

Restaurant owners and grocers always made a point of telling potential customers that they had large quantities of products in stock. C. & C. Schiller's Confectionery and Restaurant assured readers, "The proprietors of this well known Establishment beg leave to remind the citizens of St. Paul generally and strangers visiting the Northwestern metropolis, that their larder is well supplied daily with every variety and delicacy of the season." Grocers often listed not only the kinds of foods and dry goods available, but also their bulk quantities, as if to verify their claims.

Druggists sold a variety of medicines, many of which made outrageous claims for their healing powers. In an era before government regulation of the drug industry or advertising, Americans were left to experience through trial and error whether a drug or treatment was beneficial. Patent medicines with names that must have been familiar to Minnesotans in the 1850s now sound mysterious and slightly sinister, if not downright dangerous: Roger's Liverwort and Tar, Jayne's Alternative, Fahnestock's Vermifuge, Osgood's Chologogue, Fasgate's Anodyne Cordial, Moffatt's Life Bitters, Barry's Tricopherous, and Wolfe's Aromatic Schneidam Schnapps. The purpose of Wood's Hair Restorative, on the other hand, is both clear and familiar to readers today and was further explained: "This is a most astonishing preparation, and perhaps the only ever brought before the public, that will bring back the hair that has prematurely fallen."[24]

Advertisements for popular entertainment show what interested and amused territorial residents. Plays, singing, and poetry recitals were usually combined into one program and presented for a night or two at a time. In August 1857, for example, two theaters in St. Paul vied for patrons. At the People's Theatre, the play *Satan in Paris,* Mr. Jamison's recital of "Mynheer Hans Schwab's Adventure," a song by Max Irvine, and another stage piece, "Rough Diamond," were one evening's entertainment. At Scott's Theatre, the play was *Ireland As It Is,* and the program included a dance and a poem. A year earlier, Ned Davis's traveling minstrel show, advertised as "The Magnificent Floating Theatre," arrived in St. Paul to offer "a Grand Melange of Amusement upon the Palatial Steamer BANJO," capable of seating 800. The program promised to "suit the taste of all classes" with: "Songs, Ballads, National Melodies, Refrains, Operatic Melodies, Duetts, Choruses, Northern and Southern Negro Eccentricities, Dancing, Jokes, etc, etc."[25]

Cures for most ailments imaginable offered alongside butcher knives and groceries, *St. Anthony Express,* June 6, 1855, page 3.

ON MAY 15, 1858, the *Minnesotian* reported that St. Paul newspapers had been anxiously awaiting the arrival of the steamboat *Grey Eagle,* with the most recent

Dubuque Express and Herald containing news from Congress on Minnesota's application for statehood. The *Minnesotian* gleefully described what happened after the boat's arrival: "The news of admission of Minnesota into the Union spread throughout the city yesterday morning. . . . The *Pioneer* issued an extra, which it scattered through town, and the *Minnesotian Office* a large sheet handbill, in which was displayed in six inch letters, MINNESOTA IS ADMITTED INTO THE UNION."

The editor concluded his report with a personal assessment typical of Minnesota's frontier press: "Everybody seemed satisfied, that we were at last out of that '*snarl*,' and everybody said to everybody, as each drew a long breath, 'Well! what next? Good times, eh?'"[26]

Winona Times, May 15, 1858, page 2

NOTES

[1] George S. Hage, *Newspapers on the Minnesota Frontier, 1849–1860* (St. Paul: Minnesota Historical Society [MHS], 1967), 3–4, 22–23; Theodore C. Blegen, *Minnesota: A History of the State* (Minneapolis: University of Minnesota Press, 1963), 184–85.

[2] Here and below, Hage, *Newspapers*, 19, 47, 71, 138–45. The population of the territory in 1854 was 32,000; by 1857, it had grown to 150,037. William W. Folwell, *A History of Minnesota* (St. Paul: MHS, 1956), 1:360.

[3] Rhoda R. Gilman, *The Story of Minnesota's Past* (St. Paul: MHS Press, 1989), 104. An advertisement for the Prairie du Chien and St. Paul Packet Line heralded its connection to the Milwaukee and Mississippi Railroad at Prairie du Chien; *Daily Pioneer and Democrat*, May 30, 1857.

[4] Hage, *Newspapers*, 18–19.

[5] Hage, *Newspapers*, 15.

[6] Hage, *Newspapers*, 7, 8–9 (*Pioneer* quote). For more on boosterism, see William E. Lass, "The Eden of the West," within.

[7] *Pioneer*, Jan. 23, 1850, quoted in Hage, *Newspapers*, 23.

[8] *Weekly Minnesotian*, Oct. 16, 1852; *St. Croix Union*, June 16, 1855.

[9] *Minnesota Democrat*, June 3, 1851; *Minnesota Pioneer*, Jan. 14, 1851, quoted in Hage, *Newspapers*, 36.

[10] Folwell, *History of Minnesota*, 1:371–72. Rice felt that he had been wronged by Sibley and the American Fur Company. Ramsey and the other territorial officers had been appointed by the Whig administration in Washington.

[11] Hage, *Newspapers*, 26–27, 34, 138. Robertson generally supported the Rice faction and criticized Sibley and Ramsey.

[12] Blegen, *Minnesota*, 215–17; Hage, *Newspapers*, 25, 60.

[13] Folwell, *History of Minnesota*, 1:374–75.

[14] Hage, *Newspapers*, 60–62.

[15] Hage, *Newspapers*, 66.

[16] Folwell, *History of Minnesota*, 1:394; Hage, *Newspapers*, 67.

[17] *Winona Argus*, Feb. 19, 1857.

[18] Folwell, *History of Minnesota*, 1:406–11.

[19] *Minnesota Chronicle and Register*, Sept. 1, 1849.

[20] *Minnesota Democrat*, June 10, 1851.

[21] *St. Croix Union*, June 23, 1855, Apr. 18, 1856; *St. Anthony Express*, May 26, 1855; *Weekly Minnesotian*, Mar. 26, 1853.

[22] *St. Anthony Express*, Mar. 3, 1855.

[23] Here and two paragraphs below, *Daily Pioneer and Democrat*, May 30, 1857.

[24] *St. Anthony Express*, Jan. 6, 1855.

[25] *Daily Pioneer and Democrat*, Aug. 22, 1857, Aug. 4, 1856.

[26] *Weekly Minnesotian*, May 15, 1858.

# of Henry McKenty

HENRY "BROAD ACRES" MCKENTY, the king of the real estate dealers in territorial St. Paul, stood on the walk outside his office at Third and Minnesota Streets, surveying the colorful crowds moving past his corner. It was August 29, 1857, and disastrous news had reached the booming city a day earlier. In New York on August 24, the Ohio Life Insurance and Trust Company, unable to collect on its heavy loans against railroad stocks, had suspended business, setting off a panic that already had spread westward. In St. Paul, money had been tight all summer, as McKenty well knew. What little there was to lend commanded monthly interest rates of 4 or 5 percent. Now he wondered if the bubble of wild real estate speculation, with its heavily inflated prices, would burst. Ruin stared him in the face.[1]

His visits that morning to several of St. Paul's banking houses were hardly encouraging. Rumors already were circulating, fueled in part by a recent incident he had witnessed at Borup and Oakes's banking office in the Merchant's Hotel two blocks away. A well-known dry goods merchant had pushed through the crowd to beg banker Charles W. W. Borup to send $3,000 to New York immediately. Borup refused; the merchant lacked the two endorsers that the bank's rules required. The man sank into a chair, crying, "If I don't get this aid, I am ruined." McKenty was shaken, but he'd since learned that Borup had sent the merchant a note: "Your $3,000 has been sent. Never again ask for accommodations in a crowd without being ready to comply with our rules. See me privately. Yours, B."[2]

Despite the continuing excitement in the banking houses, the city today seemed serene, McKenty thought. A fierce thunderstorm two nights before had muddied the dirt streets. He watched as a long string of ox-drawn, two-wheeled carts, their axles innocent of grease, plodded along Third Street. With the arrival of the first six-cart train in 1844, Red River oxcarts had been a colorful, if noisy, accompaniment to summer in St. Paul. This season almost 500 of them had completed the 900-mile journey from Pembina. The ear-splitting squeal of their wooden axles announced their presence long before the drivers made camp on the prairie northwest of town. Now, as they passed, McKenty caught the pungent scent of their cargoes—buffalo robes and tongues, raw hides, and pemmican made of dried buffalo meat and tallow stuffed into hide bags. The *bois brulés* in their coarse blue cloth, red sashes, Indian moccasins, and profusion of brass buttons glinting in the sunlight were guiding their carts toward the warehouses of such fur-trade firms as Forbes and Kittson. The first of the carts already were being unloaded there for

transfer to some of the 15 steamboats waiting at the lower landing at the foot of Jackson Street. Profits on the cargo and the supplies that the drivers purchased for their return trip to Pembina would leave hundreds of thousands of dollars in the tills of St. Paul merchants, McKenty knew.[3]

Almost 1,000 steamboats so far this season had nosed in at the landing, disgorging hundreds of immigrants to the territory. McKenty watched as the sharpers among them, equipped with nothing more than townsite maps and packets of

One of McKenty's frequent ads, from the August 29, 1857 issue of the weekly *St. Paul Advertiser*

Métis or *bois brulés* guiding oxcarts past a saloon and building under construction
at St. Paul's Third and Washington Streets, about 1858

blank deeds, promptly set up shop on the sidewalks. Lodgings for newcomers were lamentably scarce this season. Even though 500 new buildings had gone up a year ago, he knew it was next to impossible to find a good house. The "merest shanties," the newspapers reported, rented for $8 to $10 to as much as $12 a month without water and conveniences.[4]

McKenty himself had been among the fortune-seekers when he arrived in St. Paul from Philadelphia in 1851 at the age of 30. He was proud of what he had accomplished in six years. Small, wiry, active, and genial,

he had caught the wave of prosperity of the 1850s. He remembered how he had bought several thousand acres of farmland near Stillwater for $1.25 an acre and sold it the following year for $5.00 an acre, clearing $23,000 which he immediately invested in more land. Fast-paced buying and selling of property had made him wealthy.[5]

But McKenty had other matters on his mind this August day in 1857. At home some three blocks away at Sixth and Robert Streets, his wife Johannah awaited the birth of their first child in November. This month

alone, fires had destroyed buildings nearby on Robert and Third Street, and so McKenty planned to move his family out of the city and into a house he was building on the shores of the lovely Lake Como. He already owned most of the property around the lake, and he had hired a contractor to build a road from Rice and Rondo Streets to the lake. Now completed, his Como Road, he felt sure, would help him realize his dream of creating a prime resort area. In newspaper ads headed "Como," he listed "a few Lots designed for Residences on this beautiful Lake Two Miles from city, for sale on long time" and noted that an obligation to build and improve was required of every purchaser.[6]

Surveying his own chances for surviving the current financial crisis, McKenty placed his faith in the future of St. Paul. Only last winter Joe Rolette had saved the state capital for St. Paul by the simple expedient of pocketing the bill that would have moved it to St. Peter. Five hundred men were hard at work grading the downtown streets. The state constitution was almost ready for ratification in preparation for statehood next year. Gas lights would illuminate Third Street by fall. William Markoe proposed a magnificent ascension in his new balloon, "Minnesota," as soon as $500 worth of tickets had been sold to pay for it. The People's Theatre at Fourth and St. Peter was presenting *Camille* at 75 cents for reserved seats. The World's Circus was due in St. Paul that weekend for a three-day run, and the St. Paul City Guards were planning a military dress ball in their armory for next Monday, August 31.[7] Despite the gathering financial storm, the future seemed bright for Henry McKenty.

HIS OPTIMISM *was misplaced. McKenty never recovered from the Panic of 1857. Despondent, on August 10, 1869, he shot himself. He is buried in Oakland Cemetery.*[8]

—Virginia B. Kunz

NOTES

[1] *Daily Minnesotian* (St. Paul), Aug. 28, 1857; T. M. Newson, *Pen Pictures of St. Paul, Minnesota, and Biographical Sketches of Old Pioneers* (St. Paul: the author, 1886), 322; *St. Paul Advertiser*, Aug. 8, 1857, p. 3.

[2] Newson, *Pen Pictures*, 171.

[3] *Daily Pioneer and Democrat* (St. Paul), Aug. 28, 1857, p. 3; Edward J. Lettermann, "The Trailways of History," *Ramsey County History* 8 (Fall 1971): 15–18. For more on the *bois brulé*, see Carolyn Gilman, "A Day in the Life: The *Gens Libres*," within. The campsite was near present-day University Avenue and Dale Street.

[4] J. Fletcher Williams, *A History of the City of Saint Paul to 1875* (1876; reprint, St. Paul: Minnesota Historical Society Press, 1983), 380; *Daily Minnesotian*, Aug. 27, 1857, p. 3.

[5] Williams, *History of St. Paul*, 358; Warren Upham, *Minnesota Geographic Names, Their Origin and Historic Significance* (1920; reprint, St. Paul: Minnesota Historical Society, 1969), 440.

[6] Records of Oakland Cemetery, St. Paul; Junior Pioneer Association, "The Enterprising Salesman and the Old Road to Lake Como," *Ramsey County History* 6 (Spring 1969): 14; *Daily Minnesotian*, Aug. 28, 1857, p. 2.

[7] Williams, *History of St. Paul*, 370; *St. Paul Advertiser*, Aug. 29, Sept. 19, Sept. 26, 1857—all p. 3. For more on Rolette, see Bruce M. White, "The Power of Whiteness, or The Life and Times of Joseph Rolette Jr.," within.

[8] Junior Pioneer Assn., "Enterprising Salesman," 16.

Scenic view of Lake Como, showing Henry McKenty's big brick house, partially obscured by trees, and outbuilding, about 1863

Every Object Tells a Story

MARCIA G. ANDERSON WITH
COLLECTIONS AND SITES STAFF

Buckskin coat with quill embroidery, once owned by
Governor Alexander Ramsey

I PICTURE YOU SEATED in a comfortable chair at home, reading. As you settle in, take a moment to reflect on the value of objects in your everyday life and in the telling of history. Look around and note the things that hold stories for you, that connect to your past and play a part in your life. Often, it is an object's *story*—not its intrinsic value—that pushes you to display it or keep it always close. Objects link us to the past in a way that no other medium can. People may give away file drawers full of business or personal records, books, photographs, and other printed or written material mainly because the information can be duplicated or saved in a number of formats. But when asked to consider letting go of a chair used by their great-grandparents, it's another story. That chair is a tangible object, and its owner can share an intimate experience with previous owners or users by sitting in it or simply resting a hand on the back rail.

The Minnesota Historical Society's founders, concerned about preserving the history that they were making in the midnineteenth century, began collecting objects as soon as the institution was founded in 1849. At its annual meeting two years later, its president, Governor Alexander Ramsey, shared the vision:

> A *Historical* Society in a land of yesterday! Such an announcement would indeed naturally excite at the first glance incredulity and wonder in the general mind. Well might it be exclaimed, "the country which has *no past,* can have no history"; with force could it be asked, "*where* are your records?" and if we even had them, it would not be surprising if it were still demanded, "what those records could possibly record?—what negotiations?—what legislation?—what progress in art or intellect could they possibly exhibit? Canst thou gather figs from thorns, or grapes from thistles?"[1]

Those early acquisitions reflect their collectors' and donors' ideas of what was important in Minnesota's history and culture at the time and, as a result, relate stories of individuals from the majority culture—primarily men. Later generations of curators have widened their view of what's collectable, what's valuable, and what represents the broadest experiences of Minnesota's population. Newspaper accounts from the territorial period, photographs, census records, and personal letters and journals give us some insight. Nonetheless, many of the participants in this volatile period of Minnesota's history—itinerants moving through the territory, small business owners or manufacturers, Indians and other people of color, rural folk, women, children, and families—were underrecorded in their time and remain underdocumented. As a result, we continue to look for new, imaginative ways to recreate the stories of these people's lives.

THE SOCIETY'S MUSEUM collections include approximately 250,000 three-dimensional historical objects and nearly 1 million archaeological artifacts, with good representation of the fur-trade era, Indian culture, the Henry H. Sibley and Lac qui Parle sites, early entrepreneurial activity, and the precious family treasures brought here by territorial immigrants. Many of these things can provide a tangible connection to lesser-known people from that time.

Sometimes objects come to the museum without much information, and curatorial and conservation staff must serve as historical detectives. By analyzing elements such as the materials, manufacture, and use patterns and then tying together the facts available in other resources, we can often assemble the story of an object and its makers and users, placing them all in a broader historical context. Such is the case in the story below of Sarah A. Sibley's ermine muff and tippet.

Another story included here shows what three-dimensional objects can offer when other information is lacking. The quilt squares that friends gave to Hamilton and Sarah Jane Clark(e) when they left Pennsylvania in 1852 for their new home near Shakopee are the only record we have, at present, of these settlers. If they had been in a battle, we'd have dates, illustrations, or, perhaps, newspaper accounts. Because these simple pieces of hand-sewn and signed fabric were preserved, we can ask why the Clarks traded the life of a merchant's family for that of farmers, what they looked like, and why they never assembled a quilt from the squares. We know that community was important to them and their friends in Pennsylvania; clearly, they sought to retain that sense of belonging in their new home, as they and their descendants saved the squares for well over 100 years. Questions and deductions like these make us better historians.

Some of the objects preserved by the territorial movers and shakers and cared for by the early museum staff reflect an inherent flaw in documenting one's own culture: It's hard to be objective. We tend to acquire things of personal interest. As a result, history museums have many objects now referred to as relics and curios. In the early years, the Minnesota Historical Society's gifts included these 1856 donations from Samuel Whiting of Winona: "Leaf from the large Banian Tree in the East India Co.'s Garden, in Calcutta, 1853" and "A Rose Geranium Leaf, from the Grave of Napoleon I, at St. Helena, together with some poetry in reference to it." An unknown supporter donated "A leaf from the 'Old Charter Oak,' after the tree fell, August 21st, 1856." Many of these donations were lost when the capitol burned in 1881,

and most are no longer relevant to Minnesota history or to the kinds of stories that museums preserve and share or that historians will investigate today and in the future. Even so, some of these acquisitions do reflect what types of things excited people, informed political and personal decisions, or provided a place in the world context for those who were charting new territory for themselves and their families.

ON THE OTHER HAND, much of what early Minnesota Historical Society staff collected and documented *was* important and contributes significantly to our understanding of the past. For example, Mrs. Henry Jackson-Hinchley of Mankato donated St. Paul's first post office, a small, crudely made, nondescript pine box with 12 pigeonholes for sorting mail. It was used between 1842 and 1849 by her husband, Henry, who served as postmaster. And in 1890 a St. Paulite, Capt. Charles H. Beaulieu, donated a fire steel used by "Aysh-ke-bug-e-co-zhay (Flat Mouth) Head Chief of the 'Pillager' Chippewas." The documentation of these two pieces is substantial for the time period, although curators today would have asked more questions and sought photographs, journals, and direct quotes regarding usage, the users, and the makers.

One of the most significant objects in the Society's collections from the territorial period is a rare, quill-decorated leather coat once owned by Governor Ramsey. Dating to the mid-1800s, it is modeled on the western style of cloth coat worn by Europeans of the time. The Ojibwe, Cree, Eastern Sioux, and Red River métis made this type of garment, and similar ones are portrayed in illustrations of treaty signings and other significant events of the period.

Ramsey's granddaughters, Laura and Anita Furness, donated this coat to the Society in 1943; unfortunately, records describe it only as a white buckskin scout coat (Sioux) and say nothing about how it was used, why it was saved, who made it, or where it was from. People have postulated that Ramsey bought it as a souvenir of his role in negotiating an Indian treaty, but it is just as likely that it was made and presented to him as a gift at a treaty signing or a similar occasion. Whatever its origins, curatorial and conservation staff were able to date the jacket by style and construction and can elaborate its story by determining how the skin was prepared, identifying the animal source of quills and the dye used to color them, and searching for more clues in illustrations and art of the period as well as in the voluminous records of Minnesota's first governor. Coats of this era, method of manufacture, and quality are exceedingly rare. Ramsey and his family knew that—and we can somewhat confidently assume that they preserved it because it has some tie to Minnesota history.

While many of the collections have been assembled primarily through donations, the Society has more recently taken an active role in searching out objects that illustrate the variety of the state and region. While it is unlikely that we will find significant items from the territorial period today, the last 25 years of diligent work have further shaped the already rich collections, adding depth and diversity.

As leading material-culture specialist Thomas J. Schlereth aptly wrote, "The artifacts made and used by a people are not only a basic expression of that people; they are, like culture itself, a necessary means of man's self-fulfillment."[2] The Minnesota Historical Society builds its collections to illustrate the broad and commonly shared themes of the Minnesota story as well as aspects that diverge from prevailing ethnic, religious, political, or socioeconomic norms. We hope that the objects and their stories below bring each of you a meaningful encounter with the past, one that is relevant to your everyday lives and your personal reflections on history.

—*Marcia G. Anderson*

HUNTING RIFLE

The settlement of Minnesota's frontier coincided with the nationwide transformation of gunsmithing from a craft to an industry. In the decades before the Civil War, the production of firearms by individual artisans resulted in unique weapons with stylistic trademarks representing a specific region. After 1860, large-scale manufacturing, aided by the distribution system of the railroads, began to displace independent craftsmen, and local characteristics in firearms slowly vanished.

Most of the firearms used in Minnesota Territory were handmade products from other regions and countries including New England, France, Germany, and Sweden. Minnesota's early gunsmiths were often transplanted from other countries as well. William Golcher, born in England in 1834, emigrated to Philadelphia in 1840 with his father, a prominent gunsmith. Under his tutelage, Golcher mastered the art and by age 18 became foreman of his father's shop. In 1855 Golcher moved west and opened his own establishment in St. Paul with associate James Simpson.

Golcher & Simpson produced firearms suited to the rigors of frontier life, including the half-stock plains rifle and the heavy double shotgun. The quality of the firm's workmanship was renowned, and the partnership soon developed into one of the most prolific gun trades in the Northwest. Simpson left in 1863, but Golcher operated a business in St. Paul until 1878. He later moved to San Francisco, where he managed a gun shop until his death in 1886.

Golcher & Simpson crafted this muzzle-loading hunting rifle for St. Paul entrepreneur Auguste Louis Larpenteur in the late 1850s. A magnificent example of custom-made work from one of Minnesota's pioneering gunsmiths, this .45-caliber weapon features platinum and silver fittings and a walnut stock adorned with the initials of its fortunate owner in nickel silver.

—*Adam Scher*

SLATE BOARD AND PENCILS

These slate pencils and the slate board fragment were discovered in 1940 during excavations of the Alexander G. Huggins house site at western Minnesota's Lac qui Parle mission. Huggins, according to historian Theodore C. Blegen in *Minnesota: A History of the State,* was a "lay teacher of farming" who traveled to Lac qui Parle with Dr. Thomas S. Williamson in 1835 to establish the mission for "Christianizing the Sioux." Richard R. Sackett conducted the excavations for the Works Projects Administration.

It is unusual to find 19 slate writing tools at one site. The large number suggests that school classes may have met in the residence. The slate board fragment has lines scored on one side to guide the writer and the word "Wapanton" (Wahpeton?) inscribed on the other in script. The Wahpeton division of the Dakota lived near Traverse des Sioux, Lac qui Parle, and Big Stone Lake. According to Helen Tanner's *Atlas of Great Lakes Indian History,* Traverse des Sioux was an important river crossing. Lac qui Parle was probably the best-known "civilizing" experiment among the Dakota in the 1830s; missionaries there received the support of the influential trader Joseph Renville.

—*Charles O. Diesen*

MOCCASINS

In the years preceding 1849, most Dakota villages along the St. Peter's (Minnesota) and Mississippi Rivers contained a Christian mission school sponsored by the American Board of Commissioners for Foreign Missions. For missionaries, it was not an easy decision to accept an assignment in Indian territory. Writing from her parents' home in Quincy, Illinois, in February 1848, young Nancy Hunter comforted her betrothed, the Reverend John F. Aiton: "How could Providence speak more plainly . . . it seems to speak 'Labor for the Indian.' Their souls are precious." Hunter's fiancé wrote back in March from his Cincinnati seminary: "I have been anxiously revolving our going to the Sioux, in my mind. . . . My own physical courage is *very small.* Yet the Dr. [Thomas S. Williamson] thinks that *firmness* might supply its place; but I doubt it."

The Aitons finally decided to accept a mission assignment among the Dakota at Red Wing village. By August 1848 the couple, with their modest belongings, had settled into the elm-bark village where they taught young Dakota women and men from Many Rattlesnakes' band. School ledgers show that the number of pupils varied greatly according to hunting and gathering cycles, and the Aitons occasionally served with the Williamsons at nearby Kaposia. Despite joys and fellowship, however, the trials and cultural alienation of frontier life were considerable, and after less than three years Nancy, having survived frequent bouts of homesickness and the deaths of two children, died of pulmonary consumption.

John Aiton remarried in 1855, this time to young Ohioan Mary Briggs, a missionary at Kaposia. From service there, the couple saved a pair of center-seam moccasins now in the Sibley Historic Site collection. The unworn moccasins have smoked-leather uppers, fine silk ribbonwork on the vamps and cuffs, and white seed-bead edging on the low cuffs.

The Aitons served the Dakota at Yellow Medicine and the Hazelwood Republic before settling on a farm near St. Peter. After her husband's death in 1892, Mary moved to Minneapolis, where in 1908 she organized the Captain Richard Somers Chapter of the Daughters of the American Revolution. In 1912 and 1915, Aiton contributed the moccasins and other keepsakes to the DAR's newly opened Sibley House Museum.

—*Lisa A. Krahn*

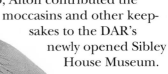

MUFF AND TIPPET

An ermine muff and tippet, or cape, offer a real-world example of the physical and cultural distance traveled by furs in the Indian trade. Henry Sibley of the American Fur Company sent the furs to his youngest sister, Sarah Alexandrine (not to be confused with his wife Sarah Jane), and the 19-year-old had this fur ensemble created for an 1840 visit to Washington City (Washington, D.C.) with her father, Michigan supreme court justice Solomon Sibley.

Each pure-white ermine pelt used in the muff and tippet has a showy dark-tipped tail; this is the winter camouflage coat of the American least weasel. The many tiny skins required for Sarah's ensemble, probably captured one by one in Indian snares in the late winter of 1838–39, were scraped clean of flesh by Indian women. The excellent quality of the furs probably brought the hunter the maximum (although still small) value in trade goods that spring. The fur company shipped thousands of packs of animal furs to the Leipzig fur markets each summer, but Sibley most likely diverted these premium pelts directly to his sister.

Fashion drawings in *Godey's Lady's Book* for the late 1830s depict ermine winter outerwear accessories, including tippets, collars, cuffs, and muffs, and Sarah probably instructed a furrier to imitate these popular designs. The beautiful workmanship of an unknown Detroit or Washington City furrier can be seen in the watermelon-pink silk linings, hand-crocheted button closures, and careful decorative arrangement of the tails. The result is a set of accessories that would be the envy of any fashion-conscious upper-class woman, east or west.

These unique objects were donated to the Sibley Historic Site collection in 1948 by Frances W. Sibley, who inherited them from her aunt, Sarah A., after her death in Detroit in 1918. The ermine ensemble has yellowed somewhat with age, but very few premium trade furs like these still exist, especially in such good condition and with such an evocative history.

—*Lisa A. Krahn*

SHIP'S WHEEL AND BELL

Christened in Washington, D.C., in 1855 with water from the Minnesota River, the *U.S.S. Minnesota* was among the last of the great wooden warships. One of the largest in the U.S. Navy when constructed, the *Minnesota* was a 285-foot, 3,200-ton, steam-driven frigate armed with 40 guns. Its first tour of duty took it to Asia as part of the East India Squadron from 1857 to 1859. With the outbreak of the Civil War, it became the flagship of the Atlantic blockade flotilla that in June 1861 captured the first Confederate warship, the *Savannah*.

Less than a year later the *Minnesota* witnessed the first encounter between armored ships in a battle that would revolutionize naval warfare. On March 8, 1862, it was serving near Hampton Roads, Virginia, when it was attacked by the *C.S.S. Virginia* (formerly the *Merrimac*), an armored Confederate vessel. The *Virginia*'s opening rounds damaged the *Minnesota*'s main mast, and afterwards it ran aground. It was spared a second attack because the *Virginia* drew too much water to advance within firing range. Nightfall halted the engagement, and in the morning the U.S. Navy's ironclad *Monitor* arrived to battle the *Virginia*. The two fired dozens of shots into each other without measurable effect, demonstrating that wooden vessels like the *Minnesota* would never be able to contend successfully with armored ships. Witnessing this first battle between ironclads, *Minnesota* commander Colonel Gideon J. Van Brunt wrote: "Never before was anything like it dreamed of by the great-

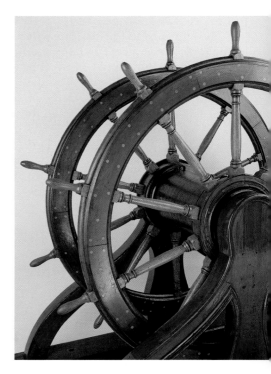

est enthusiast in maritime warfare." However, by the end of the nineteenth century, armored vessels would comprise most of the world's modern navies.

The *Minnesota* was withdrawn from active service in 1865, and for the next 35 years it served as a training vessel. In 1901 Cass Gilbert, architect of the Minnesota capitol building, persuaded state commissioners to petition the federal government to donate an artifact from the ship for display. Three years later Congress authorized the donation of the steering wheel and bell to the Minnesota Historical Society. Measuring about five feet in diameter, the double wooden wheel required two helmsmen to operate. As many as six sailors might be needed to man it in bad weather. The cast brass bell, which is 30 inches in diameter and weighs about 300 pounds, bears the *Minnesota*'s name, the initials of the Washington navy yard where the ship was built, and the year the bell was dedicated, 1856.

—*Adam Scher*

COTTON DRESS

This paisley-printed, sheer cotton summer dress was worn by a young woman, probably for her wedding or the social activities preceding it. *Godey's Lady's Book* for April 1855 describes fashionable, flounced dresses and confirms what this particular garment tells us about Lavinia Tarr, for whom it was probably made: "A handsome flounced dress is always more expensive than one with a plain skirt, and ladies of ample fortune are apt to give a preference to what only a limited number can afford to wear."

Tarr married John Freeman Norrish, both of Devonshire, England, in May 1858. Immediately afterward they sailed for the United States,

where Norrish had recently become a partner in the J. L. Thorne and Co. dry goods business in the up-and-coming town of Hastings, Minnesota. Lavinia may or may not have been a lady of "ample fortune," but she certainly had ready access to fashionable English dress goods from her husband's store.

Though little information survives about Lavinia, records show that John Norrish was a well-known businessman and public official during the 40 years he lived in Hastings. Born in 1828, he emigrated to America in 1852 and found his way to Hastings by 1857. There he not only stocked a "superior line" of dress goods, but he became a member of the state legislature in 1876 and 1881, director of the state prison, and director of the state agricultural society. He easily fits the profile of a man who could provide for a lady used to dressing in the height of fashion.

What we know of Lavinia is limited to her 1835 birth date, her 1858 marriage date, her five daughters' birth dates, recorded in census records, and the death dates of three infants, found in *Hastings Gazette* obituaries. We can guess, though, that as the wife of a prominent citizen and a resident of the only octagon house in Hastings, she must have indeed been a fashionable woman.

The muslin day dress with its flounces, paisley print, and tiny-waisted full skirt was donated by the couple's daughter in 1941.

—*Linda McShannock*

SATCHEL

Family legend has it that Samuel Ashley Higbee carried everything he needed for his new life in Minnesota Territory in this handmade wooden satchel. The inscription inside it reads: "Uncle Ashley's satchel. He carried this on a stick over his shoulder when he came from Bloomfield, Wisconsin to Minnesota. He walked the whole distance. . . . when they came in 1858 and bought land—the old Grannis farm at Vernon Center."

Higbee had moved first from Claremont, New Hampshire, to Wisconsin with his sister and brother-in-law, Caroline and Samuel Rice Grannis. Sometime during 1858, the year of Minnesota's statehood, Higbee set out for this small Blue Earth County settlement in search of unbroken sod. Higbee's sister and brother-in-law followed in 1859, and his 21-year-old nephew and namesake, Samuel Higbee Grannis, arrived in 1860.

A shoemaker by trade, Higbee probably made this satchel himself. Constructed of wood, reinforced with metal straps, and covered with oil-impregnated cloth sometimes called leatherette, the crude satchel

TIFFANY CUP

In marked contrast to the handmade satchel brought to the territory, this fancy silver cup made by New York's prestigious Tiffany and Company also found a home in early Minnesota. While we know little about how the cup—engraved with the name "Mattie" in old English letters—arrived in the territory, we can speculate based on what we know about the family that owned it.

Edmund Rice met and married Anna Maria "Mattie" Acker in Kalamazoo in 1848. Both were members of families that had migrated to Michigan from the East, she from New York and he from Vermont. The next year, like other young couples at the time, they headed west where land was cheap and opportunities seemed promising.[3]

In a 1953 reminiscence, their daughter Maria wrote that the family had lived in a log cabin on Third Street (now Kellogg Boulevard) in St. Paul until their home on Trout Brook, a small creek running into the Mississippi River northeast of the city, was built in 1862. Trout Brook was the homestead of the Rice family and their 11 children until the land was vacated in 1882 for the Northern Pacific Railway.

Edmund Rice operated a law office in St. Paul until 1855. Two years later he became president of the Minnesota and Pacific Railroad and its successors, which built Minnesota's first rail line, from St. Paul to St. Anthony, in 1862. His circumstances had improved enough for him to purchase a 45-acre tract at a cost of almost $9.00 per acre and to build an eight-bedroom, three-bath house complete with marble fire-

places brought from the East and a separate dining room for the family's servants.[4]

The lovely sterling-silver Tiffany cup dates to 1853–54, based on the mark on the bottom. At some time in the 1850s, Rice's fortunes on the rise, he might have given the cup to his wife as a present. As prestigious then as it is today, Tiffany made heavier gauge wares with a higher percentage of silver than most of its competitors. Decorated in the raised-relief repousse style, the cup is richly patterned by hand hammering from the inside. Also distinctive is Tiffany's "butler" finish, which resembles the finish achieved after years of hand polishing.

—*Kendra Dillard*

WOMAN'S WORKTABLE

"We remember, with all allowable pride, that the first payment on the lumber for the first schoolhouse [in St. Paul] was made with money earned with the needle by the ladies [sewing society]," wrote schoolteacher Harriet E. Bishop in her reminiscence of territorial Minnesota. For the early and mid-nineteenth century woman, sewing was at once part of her household duties and a means of artistic expression. Some historians contend that needlework was also political: "Women used their sewing and quilting skills to assert their agency in the world outside the home, to claim and secure for themselves more public and political space."[5]

could hold scarcely a change of clothing.

In 1960 Samuel Grannis's daughter Edith donated the satchel to the Minnesota Historical Society. The family's saga is recounted in a 1962 book in her father's own words. *New Hampshire to Minnesota: Memoirs of Samuel Higbee Grannis (1839—1933)*, in the MHS library, is unique in its details yet similar to the stories told by thousands of families who arrived in Minnesota from the East during the territorial period.

—*Kendra Dillard*

and tools, the worktable may have been the first piece of fine furniture designed specifically for females. Some tables doubled as small desks, including compartments for writing instruments and baize-covered writing surfaces.

Bishop's worktable, which dates from about 1850, is typical. The box is veneered mahogany, and the hinged lid opens to reveal a shallow well lined with birds-eye maple and originally partitioned to hold sewing tools and implements. The mirror inside the lid was probably used to increase the amount of reflected candle or gas light. Most worktables also featured a pleated-fabric storage bag hanging beneath the box, but Bishop's has a veneered semi-cylindrical drawer instead.

A label haphazardly stamped numerous times inside the lid and drawer reads "P. Schreiber/ Manufacturer and Designer/in Furniture and Bedding/Broadway [*illegible*]." It may have indicated where the piece was made. Did the worktable accompany Bishop on her riverboat journey to St. Paul in 1847? Or was it a gift from her new-found Minnesota friends? Whatever the

circumstances, there is no doubt that this worktable symbolizes the vital place that needlework held not only in Bishop's public and private lives but in those of many nineteenth-century women.

—*Patty Dean*

DRAGOON'S JACKET AND CAP

As Minnesota moved toward becoming a territory, a young soldier rode through Mexico City with General Winfield Scott's victorious American army. James Bell was escorting his celebrated commander on the route to Veracruz when a fall with his horse put him in the hospital. Soon mustered out of the army, Bell moved to the wilds of Wisconsin and Minnesota Territory, working as a riverboat pilot, among other jobs. Years later, his family donated the cap and jacket, pocket pistol, and playing cards used in the Mexican War to the Minnesota Historical Society. Private Bell hardly could conceive that his familiar old uniform would one day be unique.

The Second Regiment of U.S. Dragoons, Bell's outfit, had been organized for the Florida campaign of 1836, fighting the Seminole Indians there until 1842. Deployed west, most of the regiment later joined General Scott's Mexico City campaign in 1847. After participating in the Battle of Cerro Gordo and the assaults on Mexico City, the Second Dragoons remained on duty in the country as part of the hard-pressed U.S. Army of Occupation.

Enlisted men such as James Bell received one

Such seems to be the case with Bishop, who called the activities of the Circle of Industry, as the city's early ladies' sewing society was formally known, a vehicle of "rational, social pleasure" that would "elevate the moral tone of society."[6] Bishop was also the founding secretary-treasurer for the sewing society of the First Baptist Church. It is fitting that one of the few tangible reminders of her life is her worktable, donated to the Minnesota Historical Society in 1937 by Harriet Merrill Clifton of Evanston, Illinois.

The worktable as a piece of furniture, introduced by English designer Thomas Sheraton in his *Drawing–Book* (1791–94), quickly became popular in America. Usually made of mahogany and providing storage for needlework

woolen winter-service uniform jacket per year, along with a similar but untrimmed cotton drilling jacket, issued seasonally. Uniforms were normally made or inspected at Schuylkill Arsenal outside Philadelphia.

Bell's jacket, however, falls far below usual government standards. External edges at the front center and bottom are unfinished, with body and facing pieces simply laid together and coarsely stitched. The cream-colored domet flannel lining is crudely whipped together. Facings are roughly cut and unevenly attached. The external pocket flaps are false, and the narrow yellow worsted binding is sewn with wide running and felling stitches indiscriminately.

The dates of Bell's service in Mexico may explain the jacket's poor quality. In fall 1847 the acting quartermaster general of Scott's army had set up an extensive system in Mexico City to manufacture uniforms. Not until the next year, after Bell's discharge, were better-quality Philadelphia-made uniforms available.

This forage cap is the only known example with its original colored branch-band intact. Adopted in 1839, this style proved popular, at least compared to the leather forage cap it replaced. The folding cloth cape of Bell's cap was carefully cut off, and the lining and padding, chin strap, and original side buttons are no longer present. The Second Dragoons sometimes removed their caps' padding to create a more rakish appearance.

The decorative yellow band of 1½-inch worsted tape, crudely basted to the top and bottom of the cap band, clearly shows the shadow of and hole from the attachment loop of the now-missing company letter "G." Use of the colored band is well documented in paintings of troops serving in Mexico.

Bell's uniform offers a rare look

at the actual clothing worn by a member of the flamboyant Second Dragoons. Important to military historians, the uniform contrasts significantly with the never issued, regular-army garments of the Mexican War period in the National Museum of American History.

—*Stephen E. Osman*

QUILT BLOCKS

Friendship quilts with names of family and friends cross-stitched or written in ink on the center blocks of each square were popular parting gifts to families moving west. These quilts were most popular during the 1840s and 1850s, a time of great sentimentality, when many families moved to land newly opened to settlement.

The autograph-cross or album-block pattern was a favorite choice for friendship quilts. This set of autographed quilt blocks contains signatures by Pennsylvania relatives and friends of the Hamilton Clark(e) family, which left the community in 1852 for Minnesota Territory. The blocks are signed in ink, and some include dates and place names. Each of the 37 squares is made of a different cotton print, the variety of colors and designs available in the 1850s reflecting the increased output of New England textile mills. These one- and two-color, small-patterned prints were used for children's clothing and women's everyday dresses.

Hamilton, his wife, Sarah Jane, and their six children settled in Eagle Creek Township in Scott County, where Hamilton became

a farmer. The unassembled quilt blocks remained in the family until donated to MHS by a great-granddaughter in 1986.

—*Linda McShannock*

CARIOLE

"During the winter of 1851–52 I proceeded to England, having travelled in snow shoes from Athabasca to St. Paul's, a distance of 1,730 statute miles. Being aided by dogs for the last four hundred and fifty miles, which . . . were accomplished in ten days." So wrote Dr. John Rae, noted explorer associated with the Hudson's Bay Company, to an unknown recipient in February 1856. Rae arrived in St. Paul on February 14, 1852, having traversed the territory from Pembina by dog team. He was on his way back to England from the Arctic Ocean, where he had searched in vain for the ill-fated exploring party of Sir John Franklin.[7]

The mode of travel that Rae referred to in his letter was dog-sleighing or dog-sledging, a familiar and necessary form of transportation during Minnesota's snowy winters. The route between St. Paul and Pembina, where the population rivaled that of St. Paul and St. Anthony, had no stage line until 1859. Carioles, or one-person, flat-bottomed sleds, often were the only alternative to travel on snowshoes. Resembling an enclosed toboggan, these dog-drawn vehicles probably originated among Indian people.[8]

Whether or not the Minnesota Historical Society's cariole is indeed the one that carried Dr. Rae to St. Paul in 1852 is speculative. The 9-foot wood-and-hide "Red River train" presented to the historical society by William Gates Le Duc in November 1855 could be Rae's sled. It was in that year that the organization gained a "hall set apart in the Capitol . . . properly furnished with shelves for the reception of books and other documents," perhaps explaining an apparent delay in donating the sled. This seems to be corroborated by J. Fletcher Williams in his 1876 *History of the City of Saint Paul,* where he noted, "The 'dog-sledge' used by Dr. Rae, in his long journey over the snow, was presented by him to the Historical Society, as a memento, and may still be seen at their rooms."

While we may never know definitively, but this cariole still evokes rugged days long past.

—*Kendra Dillard*

NOTES

[1] Alexander Ramsey, "Our Field of Historical Research," in *Minnesota Historical Society Collections* 1 (St. Paul, 1872): 43–44.

[2] Thomas J. Schlereth, comp. and ed., *Material Culture Studies in America* (Nashville, Tenn.: American Association for State and Local History, 1982), 164.

[3] Maria Rice Dawson, manuscript, Christmas 1953, Edmund Rice and Family Papers, MHS.

[4] Maria Rice Dawson, "A Letter to My Grand Children About My Childhood Home, 'Trout Brook,'" typescript, 1953, Rice papers.

[5] Elaine Hedges, Pat Ferrero, and Julie Silber, *Hearts and Hands: Women, Quilts, and American Society* (Nashville: Rutledge Hill Press, 1996), quoted in *Winterthur Portfolio,* Winter 1988, p. 226.

[6] Bishop, *Floral Home, or First Years of Minnesota* (New York: Sheldon, Blakeman and Co., 1857), 101.

[7] John Rae, *John Rae's Correspondence with the Hudson's Bay Company on Arctic Exploration, 1844–55* (London: Hudson's Bay Record Society, 1953), xcv, xcvi, quoted in Curtis L. Roy to Alan Woolworth, Feb. 24, 1982, museum collections accession file 1981.11.25, Minnesota Historical Society, St. Paul; *The Minnesotian* (St. Paul), Feb. 21, 1852.

[8] Here and below, J. Fletcher Williams, *A History of the City of Saint Paul to 1875* (1876; reprint, St. Paul: Minnesota Historical Society Press, 1983), 322; *Proceedings of the Minnesota Historical Society, from Its Organization, Nov. 15, 1849, to the Admission of the State, May 11, 1858* (St. Paul: Ramaley and Cunningham, 1878), 12.

Emily Goodridge Grey

"WE DID NOT NOTICE *any difference in the service to any person. . . . Civility and kindness seemed to be in the air in those good old pioneer days."* These were the opinions of 23-year-old Emily Goodridge Grey, who joined the small African-American enclave in Minnesota Territory in the spring of 1857. A native of York, Pennsylvania, Emily was the daughter of William and Emily Goodridge; her father, a former slave, had been active in the underground railroad. In the early 1850s Emily married Ralph Toyer Grey, who moved to the new territory of Minnesota in 1855.

Emily and her two-year-old son William T. journeyed west two years later to join her barber husband.[1]

In her memoir, believed to be the first by a black pioneer in Minnesota Territory, Emily Grey described the rigors and the pleasures of nineteenth-century travel, including a problem that resonates more than a century later—flooding. She and her child made the trip from York by railroad, by steamboat, and, finally, by stagecoach to reach St. Anthony Falls where Ralph Grey awaited them. The young family became an integral part of a growing black community,

one which, according to the census, was more than 94 percent literate. In 1850 about 40 "free colored" were counted in the new territory, only one of whom lived in St. Anthony. The territory's black population grew very slowly to 259 in 1860; the tiny St. Anthony community increased dramatically in 1857 with the arrival not only of Emily and William Grey but also of eight families from Missouri, Arkansas, and Illinois.[2] Emily surely knew each one, and as she settled into her new residence one can imagine the letter she wrote to bring her family back East up-to-date on her new life.

The Jarrett House in St. Anthony (right), where Ralph Grey set up his barbering business, photographed by Benjamin Upton in 1858. A store selling iron and steel nails, groceries, and other provisions stood next door; the elegant Winslow House sits higher up the Mississippi River bank at left.

4 July 1857
St. Anthony, Minnesota Territory
To William Goodridge
York, Penna.

Dear Father—
I take pen in hand to convey my thoughts to you on this warm day. I am sorry it has taken me so long to write and let you know that William T. and I arrived safely in Minnesota, although the trip did take longer than expected due to the flooded roads in Wisconsin. Our train was forced to stop in Boscobel, where the nice people gave us meals, mostly ham and eggs, but as we were pretty hungry, it tasted mighty good. We finally were able to continue on to the steamboat landing in Prairie du Chien for the last part of the trip. William T. was such a good little traveler and amused the other passengers with his funny faces and antics.

It was so good that cousin Hamilton and his wife, Mary, were able to keep me company on the trip, as I do believe it would have been lonely traveling with only William T. Hamilton and Mary are now settled in their home in Minneapolis, and we have been able to see them several times.

Ralph has set up his barbering in a very fine hotel called the Jarrett House and is doing right well. We stayed in two nice rooms there until our little house was made ready. Our house is located in back of the hotel and used to be a barn, but after Ralph put in partitions and floors, plastered, and built a chimney, the place has a very warm feeling. Yesterday I finished putting wallpaper in the last room, which surprised Ralph because he did not know I could do such work. Now the only thing I have left to do is sew the curtains.

It will be a little while before we have all of the furniture that we need, but there are three furniture stores nearby, and we will buy a piece whenever we have the money saved

Stoneware preserve jar, missing its lid, about 1850

up and will make do with handmade things until then.

Ralph built me a fenced chicken coop and garden area, so every day I am up at dawn to feed the chickens and gather the eggs and prepare breakfast for Ralph. He has to be at his barber stand very early as there are so many traveling men at the Jarrett House who need to be shaved before they can be about their business. William T. and I spend the morning before it gets too hot tending the vegetables I planted. The weeds grow faster than the vegetables, but we will soon be enjoying fresh beans and carrots and potatoes. The tomatoes are not ripe yet. I am hoping to have an apple tree for delicious fruit pies.

My neighbors are kindness itself and have helped me in so many ways to feel comfortable in this new settlement. They promise to show me how to preserve vegetables, and I have learned new ways to bake bread from my New England neighbors. Mrs. Elizabeth Stone and Mrs. Hannah Munson are my favorite friends, and they stop by often to see how I am doing and to give me advice. They said they would help me learn to cut out and sew clothes for William T. and to knit so that I can make stockings for the family. It is hot now, but they advise

me that the winter can be very cold, so I must prepare.

There are not many colored folk here as yet and no church with which to be associated but we have been invited to join the First Congregational Church by the kindly Reverend Seccombe and his wife, and we have attended several of his services.[3] The Reverend is a God-fearing man who believes in equality and is not afraid to speak his mind, and his sermons are lively.

Have you heard from brothers Glenalvan and Wallace? Have they set about to go to Michigan yet? Has brother William decided to go with them? I know that they will be successful photographers wherever they go. Give my love to sister Susan and to yourself. I think of you each day.

Your loving daughter,
Emily Goodridge Grey

EMILY GREY TOOK *active part in civic and religious organizations in St. Anthony and Minneapolis such as the Minnesota Territorial Pioneers and church mission work. She had two more sons and a daughter, and lived in Minneapolis until her death, at age 82, in 1916.*

—*Mary D. Cannon
and Patricia C. Harpole*

NOTES

[1] Emily Goodridge Grey, "The Black Community in Territorial St. Anthony: A Memoir," *Minnesota History* 49 (Summer 1984): 47–48. The details of this story are drawn from her account.

[2] David Vassar Taylor, "The Blacks," in *They Chose Minnesota: A Survey of the State's Ethnic Groups,* ed. June D. Holmquist (St. Paul: Minnesota Historical Society Press, 1981), 73–74, 88n5.

[3] St. James African Methodist Episcopal Church of St. Anthony, also known as First African Methodist Episcopal Church, was not organized until 1863; Taylor, "The Blacks," 76.

Remnants of the Built Environment

SCOTT ANFINSON

The Ramsey Mill on the Vermillion River at Hastings, about 1865

ONE HUNDRED AND FIFTY YEARS of change have left little of Minnesota that would be recognizable to a territorial-era pioneer or Native American. The great pine forests have been cut, the tallgrass prairies are agricultural fields, and the Big Woods exists only in small patches. St. Anthony Falls, once regarded as "a landmark in the wilderness," is now a concrete spillway. The junction of the Mississippi and Minnesota Rivers, known as *Mendota* to the Dakota, is the heart of a sprawling city. The estuary of the St. Louis River, where walleyes spawned in great abundance, is an international port where thousand-foot ships take on cargoes of wheat, coal, and taconite. A grid of tar, gravel, and concrete highways covers the state. Even the sky has intrusive contrails of jet aircraft.

There are a number of places in Minnesota, however, where remnants of territorial days still exist, places where you can stand and see what Henry Sibley, Little Crow, and Hole-in-the-Day saw. There are traces of roads and trails once traveled by wooden wheels. There are houses where the night was lit only by the embers of the fireplace, tallow candles, and kerosene lamps. There are remnants of forts, prisons, mills, missions, hotels, and churches where the best and worst of Minnesota's early written history occurred.

The State Historic Preservation Office (SHPO) at the Minnesota Historical Society keeps records of the state's structures and sites that have historic value. According to SHPO records, at least 225 buildings have survived since territorial days (1849–58). Of these, about 150 are houses. The remainder are commercial, industrial, farm, and public buildings, schools, churches, military structures, fraternal-organization lodges, and even a lighthouse. Some look very much like they originally did, and some are in ruins. Most are still in their first locations, but some have been moved. Some have been restored, some are unrestored, and others, significantly rebuilt.

It is more difficult to quantify the thousands of archaeological sites from territorial days. A listing of some prominent ones—where ruins are visible, where archaeological excavations have been carried out, and those on the National Register of Historic Places—would contain perhaps 50 sites. A more complete tally would include every village, every hunting, gathering, or special-use site, and every burial ground utilized by the Dakota and Ojibwe from 1849 to 1858. It would count every log cabin or dugout site, every fur post, every cemetery, every mill site, and every road used by early white settlers.

The preservation of territorial historic properties allows us reach out and touch the past, not just read about it. It allows us to view craftsmanship from an age when handmade was the rule, not the exception. It allows us to better understand ways of life during a time when daily survival was a matter of hard work, wise choices, and more than a little good luck. A sampling

Warden's house on Stillwater's Main Street, 1972, occupied by the Washington County Historical Society

of surviving Minnesota territorial properties appears below. A complete listing can be seen in the SHPO office.*

TERRITORIAL PRISON, STILLWATER

As you drive north out of downtown Stillwater on State Highway 95, look to your left. Across from the railroad depot stand two old factory buildings in a small notch in the bluffs of the St. Croix River. If you look closely, you'll notice that parts of the notch are lined with massive stone blocks forming a u-shaped wall. If you look even more closely, you'll see ruins of masonry walls poking out of the gravel parking lot. These are the remains of Minnesota's former territorial prison.

In 1849 the first territorial legislature selected Stillwater as the prison site. Two years later, four acres were purchased in a swampy hollow near the north edge of town. The first warden, Frank R. Delano, was selected in 1853, and the first structures were erected: a prison building surrounded by a 14-foot-high wooden wall and, just south of the wall on a higher elevation overlooking the prison, the warden's house. In 1854 the first prisoners arrived. The following year, the grounds were drained and a workshop was constructed.

There are no photographs of Minnesota's first prison, so it is difficult to describe it exactly, although prison records give us the basic arrangement and materials. All of the buildings were constructed of

*SHPO maintains files of information for each of the properties described. For more on the Red River Trails, see Rhoda R. Gilman, Carolyn Gilman, and Deborah M. Stultz, *The Red River Trails: Oxcart Routes between St. Paul and the Selkirk Settlement, 1820–1870* (St. Paul: Minnesota Historical Society, 1979); on the military roads, see Grover Singley, *Tracing Minnesota's Old Government Roads* (St. Paul: Minnesota Historical Society, 1974).

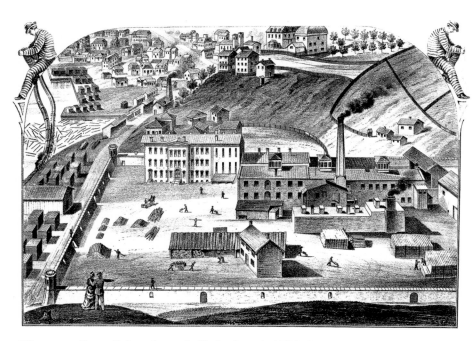

Minnesota State Prison from A. T. Andreas's 1874 *Illustrated Historical Atlas of the State of Minnesota.* **The territorial buildings stand near the river side (east); the warden's house is just outside the walls (south), at left center of drawing.**

limestone from local quarries. The main building, which contained the cell blocks, was three stories high, 45 feet long, and 30 feet wide. Nearby, within the walls, were a workshop and an office.

Until abandoned in 1914, the prison went through many changes. Major additions and new buildings were constructed in each decade. All of the original buildings except for the warden's house were torn down in 1871. The grounds were continually expanded and the walls rebuilt until the prison occupied the entire hollow. A massive stone wall completed in 1892 linked with the bedrock bluffs on three sides and bridged the gap of the hollow on the river side.

There were no famous prisoners in territorial days, at least none of such notoriety as the members of the James Gang, sent to Stillwater in 1876 after their ill-fated Northfield raid. Most territorial convicts were

thieves and murderers, both men and women. They were generally well treated but were used by area manufacturers virtually as slave labor. (Wardens were local businessmen until 1891 when the first professional penologist, Albert Garvin, was appointed.)

When a new prison was finished at Bayport just south of Stillwater in 1910, the old facility was gradually abandoned, with the last prisoners being transferred in 1914. The front wall of the prison was torn down in the 1920s, opening the first clear view to the inside from the street in nearly 70 years. In 1936 WPA crews demolished all of the prison buildings except for the shoe factory and leather warehouse.

The warden's house, the only standing structure from territorial days, is now occupied by the Washington County Historical Society. Foundations of the early prison buildings can be seen in the gravel

parking lot within the walls just northeast of this building. Caves that once stored food and other supplies pockmark the bedrock walls. Current plans are to turn the two remaining state prison buildings into a hotel.

GIDEON AND AGNES POND HOUSE, BLOOMINGTON

Along the bluffs of the Minnesota River just southwest of the foot of Portland Avenue in east Bloomington near the Mall of America is a small brick house hidden from 104th Street by a screen of trees. This house was built in 1856 by Gideon and Agnes Pond. Gideon and his brother Samuel had arrived in Minnesota in 1834 to be Christian missionaries to the Dakota. The brothers established their first mission at Lake Calhoun in what was to become Minneapolis, associating themselves with Mahpiyawicasta's (Cloud Man's) band of Mdewakanton Dakota. In 1836 Gideon went to Lac qui Parle mission in western Minnesota, where he married Sarah Poage. He returned to Lake Calhoun in 1839, but conflict with the Ojibwe was making any area north of the Minnesota River dangerous for the Dakota. When Cloud Man and his people moved south, the Ponds followed them. Gideon and Sarah established a new mission on the north bank of the Minnesota River in 1842. They called this mission Oak Grove, and there they spent the remainder of their lives.

The Ponds first built a small log building on the top of the bluff overlooking the majestic river valley. When the Dakota were forced to cede their lands west of the Mississippi River to the United States in 1851, the missionaries decided to stay at Oak Grove and minister to white settlers. They built a pre-emption cabin near the log mission, and Oak Grove became a farm. Sarah Pond died in 1853, and Gideon married Agnes Hopkins the next year. In 1856, using brick that they made themselves at a nearby kiln, Gideon and Agnes Pond built a new house adjacent to their cabin. They dismantled the mission and used the timbers to build a barn. Gideon Pond served as the minister to Oak Grove Presbyterian Church until his retirement in 1873. He died in 1878 at the age of 68. Agnes Pond died in 1915 at the age of 90.

The Pond family has continually occupied the Oak Grove site in Bloomington since 1842. Richard St. Martin, Gideon and Agnes Pond's great-grandson, still lives in the brick house, although it became the property of Bloomington in 1975. The city plans to develop the site as a historic facility, where the interpretation will extend beyond the house and the Ponds.

The Gideon and Agnes Pond house site is more than a standing structure. It is a complex of historic resources that could tell us much about territorial life in Minnesota. Archaeological loci include the mission house, the pre-emption cabin, the kiln and clay pits, and a variety of farmstead buildings. Cloud Man and his people lived on the lower terrace at Oak Grove and buried their dead on the upper terrace near the mission. Excavation of the lower-terrace village could reveal much about the Dakota during this period of great change.

Gideon and Agnes Pond, about 1854

Gideon and Agnes Pond's house, 1992

Ruins of the Ramsey Mill, about 1902

The Oak Grove site is not a place to commemorate just territorial pioneers. It needs to be a place of healing. Most missionaries who journeyed to Minnesota to minister to the Dakota and Ojibwe were good people with good intentions; they hoped to make the lives of the Indians better. In retrospect, however, by attempting to destroy Indian religion and belief systems, they did more to harm Indian culture than Euro-American soldiers and settlers. Some Dakota remember Pond's friendship. Others remember his "mission."

Gideon and Samuel Pond developed the first Dakota alphabet in 1836. Working with missionaries Stephen R. Riggs and Thomas S. Williamson, the Pond brothers published the *Grammar and Dictionary of the Dakota Language* in 1852. Gideon Pond started the first Dakota newspaper, the *Dakota Friend,* in 1850. The Ponds established close friend-ships with Dakota people. Gideon and Agnes Pond raised a loving and hard-working family in territorial Minnesota. These accomplishments are all worthy of celebration at their Oak Grove home.

THE RAMSEY AND GARDNER MILLS, HASTINGS

Minnesota once led the world in flour production. This accomplishment was not due to the state's agricultural prowess; others produced much more wheat. It also cannot be credited exclusively to the well-known mill owners in Minneapolis. The success story of Pillsbury and General Mills begins with territorial millers. It begins in southeastern Minnesota at Faribault, Dundas, and Hastings.

No visible remnants of territorial milling survive in Faribault. In Dundas, the low ruins of the first Archi-bald Mill (1857) can be seen only through careful examination of an island in the Cannon River. In Hastings, however, Minnesota's territorial flour-milling legacy is clearly visible. The high wall ruins of the Ramsey Mill stand on the banks of the Vermillion River in a city park across from the Minnesota Veterans' Home. Just upstream, the remains of the Gardner Mill are embedded in the giant Conagra Mill.

In 1856 Alexander Ramsey and Thomas Foster built a four-story limestone flour mill in the scenic gorge of the Vermillion River. They called it the Hastings City Mill, but it became known as the Ramsey Mill. By that time Ramsey had served as the first territorial governor from 1849 to 1853. Foster, a physician who had arrived in Hastings in 1851, was his close friend and political ally.

Ramsey was not involved in the day-to-day work of the mill; it was leased to operators. The business was not especially successful, particularly in territorial times. Ledger books from 1857 and 1858 reveal that it sold limited quantities of wheat flour and corn meal. When Minnesota became a state in 1858, the Ramsey Mill was one of more than 80. Ten years later, some 200 flourished in the state. Ramsey sold his interest in the mill in 1877, and it burned in December 1894. It was not rebuilt.

A smaller and earlier mill had been constructed in Hastings in 1853 on the north bank of the Vermillion River, immediately adjacent to the waterfall at the head of the gorge. Built by Harrison Graham and William Le Duc, this mill was three stories tall with a gable-roofed upper story of wood and two lower stories of limestone. Le Duc became sole owner in 1856 and enlarged the mill. Stephen Gardner bought it in 1863 and significantly rebuilt the structure, incorporating the earlier mill into the new building. It was Gardner who is credited with introducing early middlings purifiers, a milling innovation that was copied elsewhere in Minnesota. The Gardner Mill was acquired by the Peavey Company in 1928 and by Conagra in 1973 and currently is one of the most productive in the world. The remains of the earlier Le Duc and Gardner mills can be seen near its downstream end, the gable outline clear below the modern flat roof.

Citizens of territorial Minnesota knew that in order to be taken seriously by easterners they needed more than productive wheat fields and pine forests. Minnesota needed to process its resources if it were to gain national and international influence. The ruins of the Ramsey Mill, its high stone walls open to the sky, are a powerful symbol of Minnesota's past when almost every town had a flour mill.

The remains of the Gardner Mill, though more subtle to behold, have, perhaps, a more powerful meaning. The technology of flour milling had been brought to America from Europe, where centuries of wheat growing and grinding had resulted in slowly accepted innovations. The millers of southeastern Minnesota rapidly improved the process, and when these innovations were introduced into the massive mills of Pillsbury and Washburn-Crosby (General Mills) at St. Anthony Falls, Minnesota flour gained markets and respect throughout the world.

MINNESOTA POINT LIGHTHOUSE, DULUTH

The western shore of Lake Superior was sparsely populated when the Ojibwe ceded northeastern Minnesota in the 1854 Treaty of La Pointe. The fur trade had collapsed in the 1830s and trading posts had been abandoned. There were Ojibwe villages at Grand Portage, Beaver Bay, and Fond du Lac, near the mouth of the St. Louis River, and seasonal fishing stations at Grand Portage, Grand Marais, Encampment River, and, again, Fond du Lac. With the signing of the treaty, hundreds of

Gardner Mill at the falls of the Vermillion River, 1859. Its stone outline is clearly visible in the 1936 view of the Peavey mill.

Minnesota Point lighthouse and light keeper's dwelling, Duluth, about 1870

Lighthouse remains, 1970

white settlers and prospectors staked claims along Minnesota's North Shore, but when rumors of rich mineral deposits proved false and the financial Panic of 1857 hit, the tide of settlement temporarily waned.

The promise of a great port at Duluth, however, did not wane. As the agricultural fields of Minnesota and the Dakotas boomed and white pine forests yielded their great trees, eastern cities demanded the wheat and lumber. Moving products east was difficult before railroads reached the region. The Great Lakes offered an attractive water route, although the violent storms, cold water, and rocky coastline of Lake Superior were well known to sailors even in the midnineteenth century. Ways had to be found to make shipping safer.

At the mouth of Duluth harbor lies Minnesota Point, one of the longest bay-mouth sandbars in the world. In 1854 the St. Louis River swept east around Minnesota Point before it entered Lake Superior. This was the only entry into the great inner harbor at Duluth. Promoters immediately recognized the need for a lighthouse to guide sailors to the harbor entrance.

In 1855 the federal government appropriated $15,000 to build this lighthouse on the eastern end of Minnesota Point. Completed in 1858, it stood 50 feet high and was constructed of red brick shipped from Cleveland. Whitewashed mortar covered the brick to make the tower more visible. A 10-foot-high wooden turret with four large glass windows and a glass-paneled door capped it. Inside the turret was a kerosene-powered light with French-made lenses. A brick light keeper's house was constructed adjacent to the tower.

In 1870 the city of Duluth ordered a channel cut through Minnesota Point near its western end to give ships more direct access to the city's inner harbor. Although the eastern (Superior, Wisconsin) entrance grew steadily less popular, shifting sands at the east end of the point required the construction of a new light station in 1878 a quarter of a mile to the east. The lenses from the old lighthouse were moved to the new Superior entry, and the old Minnesota Point lighthouse was abandoned. The wooden turret, the interior stairway, and the light keeper's house were also removed in 1878.

Over the last 120 years the Minnesota Point lighthouse has fallen into ruin. Only 35 feet of the tower still stand, the uncovered top layers of brick gradually succumbing to the freeze-thaw cycle. A thick patch of poison ivy hampers access to the broken cylinder. Though its light is gone and its tower shattered, the lighthouse still shines bright in importance. The Minnesota Point lighthouse was the first high-powered light beacon on Lake Superior. It was a landmark that became the zero point for all of the initial surveys of the lake. It allowed safe passage into a little-known harbor at the head of Lake Superior, a harbor that is now one of the busiest in the United States.

MILITARY AND
PRETERRITORIAL ROADS
IN MINNESOTA

Present-day county lines appearing on this map
are shown for reference only.

TERRITORIAL ROADS

When Minnesota became a territory, it already had an extensive network of overland transportation routes. Most of these were Indian trails. Largely impassable by wagons, they did not necessarily make the linkages required by Euro-American settlers. What may have been the first built road in Minnesota, linking the Falls of St. Anthony with Fort Snelling, was constructed by soldiers in the early 1820s.

Cart trails were developed in the 1830s to connect Fort Snelling, the head of steamboat navigation on

the Mississippi River, with Euro-American settlements on the Red River in southern Canada. Known as Red River trails, these routes followed river valleys where possible. Major Red River trails went south from Winnipeg on both sides of the Red River and then diverged into three main routes across central Minnesota: the Minnesota Valley Trail along the Minnesota River, the Middle Trail along the Sauk River, and the Woods Trail along the Crow Wing and Mississippi Rivers. These had many spurs that offered local route options based on the weather or time of year. Red River trails fea-

tured very few improvements such as bridges, grading, or filling.

With the signing of the area's first major Indian treaty in 1837, the land between the St. Croix and Mississippi Rivers, known as the St. Croix triangle, was opened to white settlement, and the need for roads increased. Loggers developed an informal network in the triangle, linking sawmills and river landings to stands of white pine.

In the early 1850s when additional Indian treaties ceded more land, Minnesota's population began to increase rapidly, and the new settlers demanded better roads. Congress appropriated $40,000 in 1850 to construct "military" roads in Minnesota Territory; additional appropriations were passed in 1852, 1855, 1856, and 1857. Five major roads were specified in these appropriations: the mouth of the St. Croix River (Point Douglas) to the mouth of the St. Louis River (Superior); Point Douglas to Fort Ripley; the mouth of the Swan River (Little Falls) to the Winnebago Agency (Long Prairie); Mendota to Wabasha; and Mendota to the mouth of the Big Sioux River (Sioux City, Iowa). The Treaty of La Pointe in 1854 had also specified that roads be built from the mouth of the Rum River (Anoka) to Lake Mille Lacs and from the mouth of the Crow Wing River north to Leech Lake.

Surveys for the military roads began in late 1850, starting with the Mendota-to-Wabasha road. By the time of statehood in 1858, the authorized military roads had essentially been completed, although their condition and passability varied greatly. The worst section was the northern portion of the Point Douglas-to-Superior road. Like the Red River trails, the military roads followed favorable topography and existing trails wherever possible, but significant bridge building, swamp filling, and timber clearing were also done. Road beds were 25 to 50 feet in width with 100-foot cleared right-of-ways.

Local road-building initiatives were also common in territorial

Point Douglas-to-Superior Road, 1989

days. William Dodd got contributions to build a road from Traverse des Sioux (Nicollet County) to St. Paul in 1853. The Mendota-to-Big Sioux military survey crew encountered this road and drew their survey line along it. The alignment through Dakota County, still largely intact, is known today as Dodd Road. Stagecoach roads funded by private developers also began about this time, and by 1859 a network connected most towns in southeastern Minnesota.

While many territorial roads became state highways and county roads, there are not many places where the actual roads survive.

Perhaps the best example of a Red River Trail segment is on the western edge of Goose Lake Swamp in Pennington and Polk Counties. A well-preserved segment of the Point Douglas-to-Superior military road is present in St. Croix Wild River State Park in Chisago County. In Kandota Township of Todd County, off County Road 92, is a surviving segment of the St. Cloud and Red River Valley stage road.

UNLESS MAINTAINED, the built environment goes back to nature. Historic buildings become ruins, and ruins become archaeological sites invisible at the earth's surface. Walls and artifacts are precious resources. They demonstrate that the past is real, that the stories told in history books are more than stories, and that there are more stories than the books can hold. People lived in those houses, worked in those mills, traveled those roads, paced in those prison cells, and lit beacons in that tower to welcome white-winged schooners to a new world.

Territorial stories are pivotal to Minnesota history. In those 10 years, the transformation from "wilderness" to metropolis irrevocably began. The lives of native peoples, and those who came after, were changed forever. As we view those years, we must also view the present and decide what we will leave to the future. The fragile fabric of the past is a gift well worth giving.

Visiting Minnesota Territorial Sites

JOHN CRIPPEN AND KATHERINE PIVA

Territorial industries, architecture, religion, leaders, and early life are vividly portrayed at several of the Minnesota Historical Society's historic sites. In the Twin Cities area at the Sibley Historic Site, visitors can learn about Mendota's transition from an isolated trading post to part of an organized territory. Henry H. Sibley, an American Fur Company official, territorial delegate to the U.S. Congress, and leader in the quest for statehood, lived in his limestone house there until he began serving as governor of the new state in 1858. The site's Faribault house, which served as a hotel, and the Dupuis house also bear witness to the fur company's post at the confluence of the Mississippi and Minnesota Rivers.

Across the Minnesota River at Fort Snelling, the U.S. government established its presence in the decades before Minnesota became a territory. Costumed living-history interpreters now depict the residents of the 1820s.

Up the Mississippi River is the St. Anthony Falls Historic District, the site of lumber milling during the territorial years. (In those times, vistas of the roaring falls would not have included James J. Hill's Stone Arch Bridge, built in 1883.) Farther up the Mississippi River near Elk River, the Oliver Kelley family first settled in 1849, and the Society has recreated their mid-century farming practices.

For a look at residential architecture of the times, visit the W. H. C. Folsom House in Taylors Falls on the St. Croix River. Along with other homes in the Angel Hill district, it is an example of the Greek and Gothic Revival styles popular with New Englanders who settled in the area. The Folsom House was the home of the lumber baron who also served as a state representative and senator.

Near Montevideo in western Minnesota is the Lac qui Parle Mission, where missionaries founded one of the region's earliest churches and

schools. Under the patronage of Joseph Renville, missionaries developed the first Dakota alphabet and translated the Bible into Dakota. A visit today gives insights into the mixing of cultures there.

Along the Minnesota River in southern Minnesota, Fort Ridgely near Fairfax and the Lower Sioux Agency near Redwood Falls were built after the treaties of 1851 to administer U.S. Indian policy as new settlers flooded over the Dakota people's former lands and to manage government business with the small Dakota reservation along the river. For information about the impact of the territorial period on the Ojibwe people, visit the Mille Lacs Indian Museum in north-central Minnesota.

To find out about visiting these or others of the 23 historic sites administered by the Minnesota Historical Society, phone toll-free 1-888-PAST-FUN, or visit the Society's website at www.mnhs.org.

Plowing with oxen at the Oliver H. Kelley Farm

AUTHOR NOTES

MARCIA ANDERSON is chief curator of collections at the Minnesota Historical Society.

SCOTT ANFINSON is the National Register archaeologist for the Minnesota State Historic Preservation Office.

MARY D. CANNON, a staff member of the Minnesota Historical Society from 1963 until 1991, served as editor of *Minnesota History* for the last 10 of those years. Among her other publications, she co-edited with Patricia C. Harpole the annotated *Minnesota Territorial Census, 1850.*

JANE LAMM CARROLL is assistant professor of history at the College of St. Catherine in St. Paul. Her publications include "Native Americans and Criminal Justice on the Minnesota Frontier" and "Police, Press, and Public: Law Enforcement in Territorial St. Paul" in *Minnesota History,* Summer 1996 and Fall 1993, respectively.

JOHN CRIPPEN is an administrator in the historic sites department at the Minnesota Historical Society.

PATTY DEAN is the supervisory curator of museum collections at the Minnesota Historical Society.

CHARLES O. DIESEN is a museum collections curator at the Minnesota Historical Society.

KENDRA DILLARD, now in California, was a museum collections project specialist at the Minnesota Historical Society.

CAROLYN GILMAN is the author of five books and a dozen articles on Indian and fur trade history. She works for the Missouri Historical Society, where she is currently developing an exhibition on the Lewis and Clark expedition.

RHODA R. GILMAN held a variety of positions on the staff of the Minnesota Historical Society between 1958 and 1992. She has written several books and many articles on upper Midwest history and is currently at work on a biography of Henry H. Sibley.

PATRICIA C. HARPOLE, a retired librarian from the Minnesota Historical Society, was a staff member from 1963 to 1993. She is currently a freelance historical researcher and indexer.

BRIAN HORRIGAN is an exhibit curator at the Minnesota Historical Society.

LISA A. KRAHN is the site manager of the Sibley Historic Site.

VIRGINIA BRAINARD KUNZ is editor of the Ramsey County Historical Society's quarterly magazine, *Ramsey County History,* and author of 15 books on Minnesota and American history, including *St. Paul, The First 150 Years* (1991).

WILLIAM E. LASS is professor of history at Minnesota State University, Mankato. His most recent book is a second edition of *Minnesota: A History* (New York: W. W. Norton, 1998).

LINDA MCSHANNOCK is a museum collections curator at the Minnesota Historical Society.

STEPHEN E. OSMAN is the site manager of Historic Fort Snelling.

KATHERINE PIVA is a program associate in the historic sites department at the Minnesota Historical Society.

SARAH P. RUBINSTEIN is an editor for the Minnesota Historical Society Press.

ADAM SCHER is a museum collections curator at the Minnesota Historical Society.

ANTON TREUER is Leech Lake Ojibwe and an assistant professor of history at the University of Wisconsin-Milwaukee.

DAVID TREUER is Leech Lake Ojibwe and a visiting lecturer in English at the University of Wisconsin-Milwaukee.

BRUCE M. WHITE is an ethnographic historian whose numerous publications include "Indian Visits: Stereotypes of Minnesota's Native People" (*Minnesota History,* Fall 1992) and "The Woman Who Married a Beaver: Trade Patterns and Gender Roles in the Ojibwa Fur Trade" (*Ethnohistory,* forthcoming).

HELEN MCCANN WHITE, editor of *Ho for The Gold Fields* (1966) and author of *Tale of a Comet* (1984), is also the editor and publisher of the annual *Dalles Visitor* (Taylors Falls, Minnesota, and St. Croix Falls, Wisconsin). With her son, Bruce M. White, she coauthored "Fort Snelling in 1838. An Ethnographic and Historical Study" (1998).

ANGELA CAVENDER WILSON, or Tawapaha Tanka Win (Her Big Hat Woman), is the great-great-granddaughter of Maza Okiye Win. She is a Wahpetonwan Dakota residing at the Upper Sioux community in Granite Falls, Minnesota, and a doctoral candidate in American history at Cornell University.

CREDITS

The illustration facing the preface, a detail of Seth Eastman's *Mendota from Fort Snelling,* is in a private collection, courtesy the Minnesota Historical Society; p. 24 is courtesy the Royal Ontario Museum, Toronto, Canada; p. 49, the Smithsonian Institution, Washington, D.C.; and p.104 (top), the Northeast Minnesota Historical Center, Duluth. Tha bank note, p. 13, was purchased with funds donated by W. G. Kirchner. The painting on the cover and p. 8–9, from the Governor's Reception Room in the Minnesota State Capitol, was photographed by Jerry Mathiason.

All other illustrations are in the collections of the Minnesota Historical Society. The photographs on p. 6, 20, 26–27, 33, 41, 47, 53, 57, 68, 73, 86, 90 (bottom), and 98 are by Eric Mortenson/MHS; on p. 12–14, 16, 20, 48, 56, 64, 67, 70–71, 74, 88, 89, 90 (top), 91–95, and 97 are by Peter Latner/MHS; p. 101 (bottom) is by Scott Anfinson; and p. 106 is by Demian Hess. The maps on p. 4, 7, 10, and 18 are by Alan Ominsky; the one on p. 105 is from Grover Singley, *Tracing Minnesota's Old Government Roads* (St. Paul: Minnesota Historical Society, 1974).